D1196036

ACQUIRING PARKS AND RECREATION FACILITIES THROUGH MANDATORY DEDICATION: A COMPREHENSIVE GUIDE

Ronald A. Kaiser, J.D.
Attorney and Assistant Professor
Texas A&M University
College Station, Texas

and

James D. Mertes, Ph.D.
Professor, Department of Park
Administration and Landscape Architecture
Texas Tech University
Lubbock, Texas

NEW DIRECTIONS IN LEISURE

The New Directions In Leisure Series is based upon the recognition that recreation, park and leisure services are in a period of fundamental change and must respond quickly. While leisure is becoming a more important part of life, the organizations providing leisure services are being challenged to leap, not into the future, but into the present. Doing this will require new ideas and a better information base.

Copyright © 1986 Venture Publishing, Inc.
1640 Oxford Circle, State College, PA 16803

Design by Susan Lewis
Cover Design by Sandra Sikorski
Production Assistance by Bonnie Godbey

Library of Congress Catalogue Card Number 86-50112
ISBN 0-910251-13-4

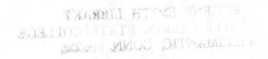

To my sons Curtis and Scott. —RK—

To my wife Jill and daughters Tiffany, Taryn and Tawny. —JM—

TABLE OF CONTENTS

CHAPTER THREE   LEGAL ISSUES IN PARK LAND DEDICATION

CHAPTER FOUR   THE PARK AND RECREATION PLAN

CHAPTER FIVE   ORDINANCE CRITERIA AND CONSIDERATIONS

CHAPTER SIX SPECIAL PROBLEMS AND OPPORTUNITIES

PREFACE AND ACKNOWLEDGEMENTS

Legal challenges to the practice of requiring subdivision developers to dedicate park land to the municipality as a precondition to approval of the subdivision plat first appeared in the 1930's. From the first efforts in the state of New York, the practice slowly was tried in other states. Judicial notoriety for the concept was raised in an Illinois case in the 1960's. After that case the practice spread to other states experiencing rapid population growth or urbanization. The practice was justified as a way to transfer the costs associated with acquiring and developing neighborhood parks to the developer whose activities generated the need for additional parks.

Exacting park land from subdivision developers has not been without political and judicial controversy as demonstrated by the case law challenging this municipal practice. Numerous law review articles have focused on some particular phase of this practice but none have comprehensively discussed the subject. The authors' many conversations with municipal officials and real estate developers have reinforced the need for a definitive work dealing exclusively with "mandatory dedication of park land through the subdivision approval process."

We have endeavored to bring into focus a definitive statement of the law, planning principles and nuances of park land dedication ordinances, practices and administration. As such, this book is not a text but a practical guide for those involved in subdivision development and regulation. The interested parties include; planners, landscape architects, park and recreation directors, attorneys, planning commission members, municipal officials, real estate developers and subdividers.

We have attempted to define the legal parameters of municipalities in developing, drafting and administering a mandatory park land dedication ordinance. Particular attention is directed to Chapters Three and Five relating to legal issues and ordinance drafting. Despite our strong support for the practice we believe that the presentation is fair, objective and comprehensive.

Mandatory dedication is not a panacea for acquiring public parks and recreation facilities. Its' application is limited to neighborhood parks and it is but one acquisition method for the park and recreation department. An exclusive reliance on this technique would not be a propitious public policy.

The authors are grateful to the many municipal officials from around the country who provided copies of their park land dedication ordinances used in this book, especially David Reed, Manager, Management Services, Park and Recreation Department, Austin, Texas. We would like to thank David Rockefeller for research assistance; Rusty Reid for creative graphics; Sharon Pope and Dottie Novosad for typing parts of the manuscript and especially Lisa Randolph, who was responsible for typing the manuscript for submission to the publisher. The manuscript was skillfully edited and improved by Sharon Kelly and we are grateful for her efforts.

A number of reviewers provided helpful comments and their contribution is appreciated. Among the reviewers were James Fletcher of California State University @ Chico, Department of Recreation and Parks Management and Frank Skilleran and Bruce Kramer of the Texas Tech University School of Law.

And we would especially like to express our appreciation to Texas A&M University, Texas Agricultural Experiment Station and Texas Tech University College of Agricultural Sciences and School of Law for creating the scholarly environment to enable us to write this book.

Ronald A. Kaiser   James D. Mertes
College Station, Texas   Lubbock, Texas

CHAPTER ONE

Mandatory Park Land Dedication: An Overview

§1.1. A Focus On the Problem

Dramatic demographic changes over the past 25 years have forced a reassessment of the traditional means of acquiring public park and recreation areas. As population growth has strained public coffers and challenged fundamental ideas on funding for parks, public officials have experimented with alternatives to the negotiated purchase of park land.

Within metropolitan areas, except for scattered "gentrification," the rush to the suburbs has been overwhelming. While the suburbs were gaining population, the central cities were losing people. Between 1970 and 1978 the white population of central cities in the U.S. decreased at an annual rate of 1.2 percent or about 5 million residents.[1] Along with the suburban growth there has been a "sunbelt" migration from the Northeast and Midwest to states in the South and West.

Rapid population growth in suburbia and migration to the "sunbelt" states have exerted intense pressure on local governments' financial capability to provide roads, schools, sewers, parks and other facilities demanded by the new residents. Often municipalities and counties have lacked the financial resources to match the growth rate while maintaining quality services. The traditional taxing or bonding mechanisms, as a means of spreading the cost of new growth to all residents, have undergone serious review. The theory that all citizens in the municipality should share in the cost of capital improvements has been replaced by a proposition that the burden of growth-induced capital expenses should be borne by those who generate the need for them.[2]

Wherever population growth has overtaxed the financial resources of local government, the development of cost shifting devices has occurred. The nation's most populous states—California, New York, Pennsylvania, Texas, Illinois, Ohio, Michigan, New Jersey and Florida—have all experimented

1

with such cost shifting. The development of these devices has created legal and political turbulence, but local governments have persisted in attempting to shift the cost of capital improvements to new residents. It is within this context that the concept of mandatory dedication of park land has evolved.

§1.2 The Mandatory Dedication Process

The requirement that a subdivision developer dedicate land to a municipality for a neighborhood park, consistent with the need for the park generated by his subdivision activity, is one of the cost shifting devices used under the umbrella of local subdivision controls. Subdivision controls are part of the local land-use control system. Their use predates zoning and unlike zoning regulations, which control the pattern of land uses, subdivision regulations control land development. The purposes of subdivision controls can be categorized into four areas. They are intended to (1) regulate the division of land into smaller parcels, (2) simplify the legal description of and recording of property, (3) supervise the control and layout of streets, utilities and parks in the subdivision to insure the orderly development of the municipality, and (4) transfer the cost of capital improvements from the city to the new residents. These controls prevent haphazard development and help insure that residential neighborhoods are properly designed by incorporating street layout configurations and other facility design and safety standards into the subdivision development process.

The design standards and development criteria for residential subdivisions are specified in the subdivision control ordinance. Typically the ordinance requires subdividers to provide streets and other public facilities, including parks, within the subdivision. These requirements are imposed as exactions or preconditions that must be met before the municipality will approve the final plat. Most subdivision control ordinances provide for a review process whereby municipalities scrutinize the plans of new residential subdivisions to determine whether they comply with the ordinance's design and safety standards for roads, utilities, parks and other improvements. This process usually begins with a conference between municipal officials and the land developer. A sketch plan or general map of the subdivision is prepared and the officials provide guidance as to whether the developer's plans conform to the standards. The subdivider incorporates these standards into the preliminary and final subdivision plats. After municipal approval, the plat is recorded and lots in the subdivision may be offered for sale.

Under the terms of a mandatory park land dedication ordinance, a subdivider is required to deed a portion of land, or its equivalent cash value, to the municipality for use as a public park. Most ordinances also allow the developer to make cash payment in-lieu of dedicating land to the city. The amount of cash fee is based on the need generated by the subdivision for neighborhood parks and the city must spend the money for parks that benefit the subdivision.

§1.3 Legal Challenges and Judicial Attitudes

Municipalities rationalize subdivision control as a legitimate exercise of police powers.[3] From a developer's viewpoint, however, the imposition of any excessive regulation under the heading of subdivision control can adversely affect the profitability of the subdivision development. This is particularly true of a prohibition against recording a subdivision plat unless certain lands are dedicated to the city for a park. It is not surprising that developers in many states have challenged the legality of park land or cash in-lieu exactions claiming that they are unconstitutional as a taking of private property for public use without compensation. The conflicts presented between public needs and private interests have resulted in a conflicting body of case law as state appellate courts have applied different standards to justify or limit the use of park land exactions. The cases addressing the validity of mandatory park land dedications or fees in-lieu of land agree on two points: there must be valid statutory authority before a municipality may impose the exaction and the exercise of this authority must not violate constitutional standards. Because the United States Supreme Court has not ruled directly on this issue, the legal limits of mandatory park land dedication remain within the purview of state courts.[4]

Municipalities are corporations created by the state and have only those powers explicitly granted by enabling legislation or implicitly derived by court interpretation of that legislation. The general power of a municipality to exercise control over subdivision and development of land is therefore derived from state legislation. This enabling authorization may be granted through home rule, or general planning and zoning legislation. Since few state statutes explicitly grant municipalities the authority to impose park land exactions in the enabling act, the question of legal authority frequently arises.

The postures taken by various state courts on the statutory authority issue have led to conflicting results. A majority of the states adhere to a liberal statutory construction rule. This rule recognizes that "it is impractical for statutes to spell out to the last detail all of the things city government must do to perform the functions imposed on them by law;" therefore, courts imply these powers from a broad reading of the statute.[5] State courts following this rule have generally found authority for mandated park land exactions in the planning and zoning legislation.

Those states that do not follow a liberal interpretation rule follow its logical counterpart: the strict construction rule. Under this rule, unless the enabling statute explicitly grants the authority for a park land exaction, a municipality may not impose the requirement. States following this rule rarely find implied delegation of authority from land use legislation.[6]

Independent of the enabling authority issue is a second consideration: the ordinance must meet the police power "reasonableness" test. This reasonableness test is a constitutional prerequisite pertaining to the method and manner used in implementing a municipal park land dedication exaction. The theory underlying the imposition of reasonable exactions is that the subdivision developer should be required to assume only those costs related to his activity that would otherwise be cast upon the general public. Costs imposed on the developer exceeding the benefit received from his activity may be unreasonable. The United States Constitution and all the state constitutions prohibit the imposition of unreasonable conditions on land developers.

State courts have provided three tests which can be used to measure the reasonableness of municipal mandatory park land dedication requirements. They are (1) the "specifically and uniquely attributable" standard[7], (2) the "rational nexus" standard[8] and (3) the "reasonably related" standard.[9] These standards outline the criteria to be used by the court in determining whether the exaction is reasonably related to public health, safety and welfare and whether the burden cast upon the developer is related to his activity.

The most restrictive, and criticized test is the "specifically and uniquely attributable" standard developed by the courts in Illinois. Under this test municipalities can exact from the developer only that amount of land that will exclusively serve the development. As stated by the Illinois court, the attribution must be virtually 100 percent, thus this rule tends to favor developers. In contrast, the "rational nexus" and "reasonably related" standards tend to favor the regulatory authority. These standards require only a modest connection between the dedication and the park needs created by the developer's activity. The proportion of attribution can range from 10 to 100 percent.

The necessity for a comprehensive park and recreation plan to guide the park land exaction process is also important, although it is not raised as frequently as the ultra vires and constitutional issues. The majority view has been that land use regulations may "precede" the development of and not be "consistent with" the comprehensive plan but this view is changing. There is a trend toward greater judicial recognition of the importance of the comprehensive plan as a defense against allegations of "unreasonableness of regulations" or "taking of property without compensation."[10] In the context of mandatory subdivision exactions of park land or fees in lieu thereof, the park and recreation plan can be used to prove the reasonableness of the exaction. A poorly prepared plan or, worse yet, no plan at all, is a standing invitation for a developer to allege that the exactions are whimsical, arbitrary and capricious and not in conformity with reasonable municipal actions.

Judicial doctrine on subdivision controls, particularly mandatory park land dedication is developing but not to the extent of zoning law. The bellwether states providing judicial direction are California, Florida, New Jersey,

Texas and Utah. The decided trend is to uphold the concept of mandatory dedication of park land.

§1.4. State Subdivision Control Variations

While all states authorize municipalities to control subdivision development, the regulating provisions vary greatly from state to state. In this section we seek to spell out some of the general rules, recognizing that an enumeration of variations is beyond the scope of this book. A listing of state subdivision control legislation is presented in Appendix B and although every attempt has been made to provide an accurate compilation, the official state statutes should always be consulted for current information.

It has been universally recognized, under either a privilege or police power theory, that the subdividing of land may be regulated by the state directly or this authority may be granted to municipalities.[11] In determining the rights of municipalities to regulate subdivision activity, attention must always be directed to the substantive and procedural requirements of the state enabling statute. Municipalities must conform to specific statutory dictates and may not deviate from these requirements, unless authorized by statute.

Subdivision regulations may properly prohibit the filing of a plat until it has been approved by the appropriate municipal authority. The municipality may prescribe the process for approval and impose conditions as a prerequisite to the approval of subdivision plats. The approval process varies among the states as to the role of the planning commission and the municipal council in preliminary and final plat approval. There is also variation in the detail of maps and engineering drawings and in the documentation required.[12] The procedure and form of park land exactions also vary. While not an exhaustive listing, the following conditions are generally imposed in a standard regime for mandatory dedication of park land: (1) a required land allocation calculated either as a percentage of land in the development, or as a population based formula; (2) a required payment of a cash fee in-lieu of a land requirement; (3) both land and a fee; (4) standards as to the minimum amount of acreage acceptable; (5) criteria regarding the suitability and location of the park site and (6) credit given to the developer for private park areas within the development. In addition to conditions imposed on the developer a number of municipalities have self-imposed conditions for the use and development of the parks or cash exacted from the developer. The following are the commonly imposed requirements; (1) the fees collected by the municipality must be spent for park development within the development area, (2) the fees must be spent within a reasonable time, or be returned to the developer or to the subdivision residents, and (3) any dedicated park land will be developed by the city within a reasonable time period.

§1.5. Organization of the Book

This book is intended to serve as a practical reference for those players involved (1) in the land development process and (2) in providing public park and recreation facilities. It provides an introduction to the major principles in the rapidly evolving practice of imposing park land exactions on subdivision developers. The book builds upon a descriptive summary of the legal doctrines and judicial opinions that form the foundation for the practice and concludes with pragmatic suggestions for drafting a municipal ordinance.

Footnotes to relevant court cases and planning guidelines are provided at the end of each chapter. The appendices include a listing of state case law and legislation, law review articles and park acreage standards. Sample ordinances are also included. These serve as illustrations and should be tailored to each particular municipality's needs. The presentation of topics in the book is straightforward. Chapter Two explains the mandatory dedication process in the context of land use law and subdivision controls. It also outlines the advantages and disadvantages of park land dedications. Chapter Three discusses the legal issues involved in the process and offers suggestions on avoiding legal pitfalls. Chapter Four discusses the comprehensive park and recreation plan and its role in the park land exaction process. Chapter Five deals with ordinance language and criteria addressing specific legal issues raised in Chapter Three. It incorporates a representative sample of ordinance language that has overcome legal challenge. The concluding chapter identifies special problems and issues that warrant further attention.

Finally, a word on terminology. To simplify the textual presentation, municipality is used interchangeably with local government. The terms are intended to include cities, villages, boroughs, counties and townships. The word "mandatory" is used to describe a required exaction imposed on the developer. It is a harsh word that may evoke a passionate response from some public officials who seek to soft pedal the concept. Nevertheless, its use is intended to indicate a compulsory requirement.

CHAPTER ONE NOTES

1. U.S. Bureau of the Census, Statistical Abstract of the United States, 1979 @ 17 (100th ed. 1979).
2. See generally Jacobsen and Redding, *Impact Taxes: Making Development Pay Its Way,* 55 N.C.L. Rev 407 (1977) and Juergensmeyer and Blake, *Impact Fees: an Answer to Local Governments' Funding Dilemma,* 9 Fla. St. U.L. Rev 415 (1981).
3. Johnston, *Constitutionality of Subdivision Control Exactions: The Quest for a Rationale,* 52 Cornell L.Q. 871, 876 (1967).
4. Ellickson, *Suburban Growth Controls: An Economic and Legal Analysis,* 86 Yale LJ. 385, 471-72 (1977).

5. *Call v. West Jordan,* 606 P.2d 217, 218-19 (Utah 1979).
6. See, *Ridgemont Development Co. v. City of East Detroit,* 100 N.W.2d 301 (Mich 1960), *Crossroads Land Co. v. City of Montgomery,* 355 So.2d 363 (Ala 1978).
7. *Pioneer Trust and Savings Bank v. Village of Mount Prospect,* 176 N.E. 2d 779 (Ill 1961).
8. *Jordan v. Village of Menomonee Falls,* 137 N.W.2d 608 (Wisc 1965).
9. *Associated Home Bldrs. of Greater E. Bay, Inc. v. City of Walnut Creek,* 484 P.2d 606 (Calif 1971).
10. Daniel Mandelker, *Land Use Law* (Charlottesville: The Michie Co, 1982), pp. 57-64.
11. E.C. Yokley, *Law of Subdivisions,* 2nd ed. (Charlottesville: The Michie Co, 1981), pp. 14-15.
12. For a comprehensive discussion of the subdivision control process, see Yokley, Supra, pp. 196-379.

CHAPTER TWO

The Mandatory Park Land Dedication Process

Several players are involved in the land development process, including developers, builders, real estate agents, bankers, attorneys, municipal planners, and the planning commission and elected officials. The developer relies on the technical advice and services of accountants, architects, attorneys, bankers, builders, contractors, engineers, landscape architects and tax consultants for guidance through the regulatory maze often involved in land development. In nearly every urban area of the United States the developer must discover and comply with a complex array of state and local building codes, zoning regulations and subdivision controls that in composite form the basis for public land use regulation. Correspondingly, the municipality uses not only the services of many of these same professionals but also relies on input from planners and park and recreation administrators in fulfilling its planning and regulatory responsibilities. The city official seeking to draft, or implement a park land dedication ordinance confronts many problems, including the need to understand the legal context in which the ordinance is construed and administered. To understand this framework, the official must have a clear picture of the interrelationship between municipal planning and land use controls.

Public land use controls did not spring forth with the baby boom of the 1950's but evolved from the common law of nuisance. Prior to the early 1920's a property owner could develop land in any way which did not cause a substantial and unreasonable interference with the use of neighboring property or violate a deed restriction placed on the land by prior landowners. As a result, most urban areas sprawled across the landscape following the developer's "own sweet will." Beginning in the 1920's, public land use controls were instituted through municipal building codes and zoning ordinances. In 1926, zoning was approved by the United States Supreme Court in the landmark case of *Village of Euclid v. Ambler Reality Co.*, 272 U.S. 365 (1926). After this case, American land use law underwent a transition that some have called the "quiet revolution."[1] Since that time the miscellany of land use

8

regulations has expanded to match the growth of urban America. Initially these regulations were the domain of municipalities but under the rubric of environmental controls the federal government has begun to regulate public land use.[2] This will be discussed later in the chapter. Mandatory dedication of park land fits into this complex web of land use regulations under the title of subdivision control.

A. COMPREHENSIVE PLANNING

Comprehensive planning is a predominant exercise of local government, although variations of it are practiced by all levels of government. The municipal planning department is the standard agency of most cities and even those cities which do not have such an agency retain private planning consultants to provide these services. A prime responsibility of this agency is to prepare a comprehensive community development plan, which is often called a "master plan," a "land use plan" or a "city plan." In the interest of uniformity it will be referred to here as a comprehensive general plan.

Definitions of comprehensive planning are as diverse as the professions dealing with the subject. To the architect comprehensive planning is city designing, to the economist it is an external modification of free market competition, and to the lawyer it is an exercise of public authority for the purpose of promoting the health, safety and welfare of the community.[3] A common theme in these definitions is that planning is a process, requiring a team effort by technical as well as lay persons.

Every state has legislation which delegates planning authority to some or all of its municipalities, though some do not have very detailed enabling acts.[4] Most of this legislation specifically authorizes the preparation of a comprehensive plan. The authority of the park and recreation director to prepare a comprehensive park and recreation plan should be ascertained prior to instituting the planning process. In some states, this responsibility is delegated to the planning commission rather than the park and recreation commission.

From time to time questions arise as to the legal effect of the comprehensive plan. As a general rule, a comprehensive plan is not self-implementing; it requires a companion regulatory program. Thus a comprehensive plan, unless expressly provided for in legislation, has no regulatory effect. A comprehensive plan is a guide to community development rather than an instrument of land use control. As stated by one court, a comprehensive plan does not control the zoning ordinance; rather, it should be reflected in the zoning ordinance.[5]

B. LAND USE CONTROLS

Sovereignty is the cornerstone of all governmental controls. It relates to political legitimacy and is the aggregate of powers essential for the functioning of a government structure. Sovereignty is manifested in the power to tax, to spend, to exercise eminent domain and to regulate human activity and resources within a given jurisdiction. Sovereign powers are vested in the federal government and in the states. Municipalities are not sovereign and only possess those powers granted by the state through constitutional provisions or enabling legislation. Under the sovereign umbrella of (1) taxation, (2) eminent domain, and (3) police power, states have given municipalities a panoply of land use control techniques. (See Figure 2-1.) While the police power is the basis for most land use controls, taxation, eminent domain and the spending power are also used to regulate land development. Taxation affects development in a number of ways. For example, housing is subsidized by income tax deductions for mortgage interest and preferential taxation for agriculture encourages the retention of open space. Public acquisition of private property through the power of eminent domain offers a means to influence private uses of land by converting the land to public use. Each of these powers—taxation, eminent domain and police power—will be described in further detail in the following sections.

§2.1. Taxation

The power to tax is the power to control and nowhere is this more evident than in taxation as a land use control device.[6] The power of taxation is the power of a sovereign state to require from individuals a contribution of money as their share of any public burden. The constitutional provision that private property shall not be taken for public use without just compensation applies only to eminent domain and is not applicable to taxation.[7] However, taxation may be a "taking" if it is not constitutionally authorized or if it is used for other than a public purpose.

A major problem with taxation as a tool of planning is its lack of precision. Most taxes are gross in effect rather than precise. For example, preferential taxation for historic structures affects all such buildings in the taxing jurisdiction and is not an apt device to affect development in a particular place. Taxation is not limited to the ad valorem, or property tax, but includes special assessments and income taxation.

Income Taxation. No detailed discussion is needed to illustrate the fact that federal and state income taxation affects land development. For example, the capital gains feature of income taxation affects how long property can be held and it may lead to speculative investment in land around the urban fringe. Favored tax treatment is available to landlords who rehabilitate substandard housing occupied by low income tenants or to those who rehabilitate historic structures into office buildings. These are only some of the ways federal and

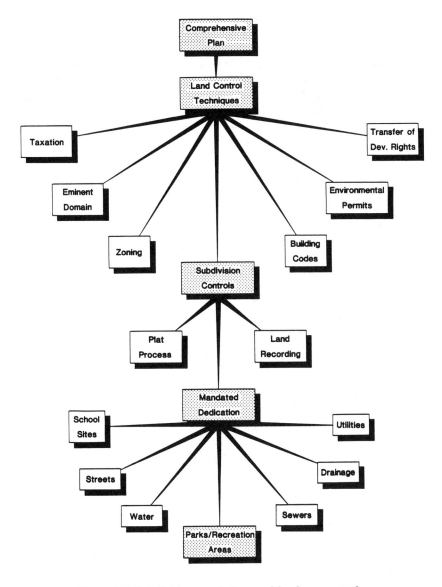

Figure 2-1 Subdivision regulations and land use controls.

state tax policies affect urban development. The numerous tax treatments seldom match local plans and regulations and may actually "overpower the ability of local government to control development."[8]

Property Taxation. Attention in the land use context has focused on the reduction of real property taxes to preserve undeveloped land or to encourage redevelopment of land. Most state laws require that real property shall be valued for tax purposes at full market value for the "highest and best use" of the property. This form of "Economic Darwinism" encourages land speculation in the urban fringe by requiring that agricultural land or open space be valued at its speculative rather than present value. Attempts to protect agricultural land from undesired speculation follow one of two approaches: either (1) the market value of the land is reduced or (2) the land is taxed at its current use value rather than its highest and best use for development. Under either approach preferential tax relief is granted to agricultural land or open space as an economic incentive to control the use of the land. Forty-four states have passed legislation to preserve agricultural land by authorizing "use valuation" as the method to calculate property taxes.[9] These laws vary in particulars as to minimum acreages, definition of agricultural uses, use value determination and penalty provision, but they all result in a lower property tax for the landowner.

Differential property taxation is a land control device with laudable goals but a mediocre track record. Studies have concluded that agricultural use valuation laws reduce the landowner's taxes, but only prevent development of land in about 1 percent of the cases.[10] Probably because it is the "cheapest" form of tax relief to farmers and suburban hobby farmers, the practice of preferential taxation will continue.

§2.2. Eminent Domain

Eminent domain is an inherent attribute of sovereignty and refers to the power of the state to take private property for public use, without the owner's consent, conditioned upon the payment of just compensation.[11] This power is inherent in the state so that recognition of it is not required in a state constitution.[12] The power of eminent domain is exercised through a process called condemnation. Municipalities, through state enabling legislation, may exercise the power of eminent domain as a land control measure.

The exercise of the power is subject to all the conditions found in the federal and state constitutions. The limiting federal provisions are (1) that private property shall not be taken for *public use* without just compensation, and (2) that no person shall be deprived of property without due process of law. In condemnation actions it is generally accepted that the municipality must establish "public necessity" for the acquisition and that the failure to establish "necessity" prevents exercise of the power. It is also generally accepted that municipalities may use condemnation to acquire land for schools, streets, utility corridors, *parks,* bridges, slum clearance, offices, libraries, cemeteries, and water supply systems. The power is not restricted to land; buildings may also be acquired.

§2.3. Police Power

Under our form of government the respective sovereign powers are listed in the federal and state constitutions. The federal government is a sovereign of "limited" powers—limited to those "express powers" enumerated in the constitution or to those "implied" from the "express" powers by the "necessary and proper clause." Thus, the Constitution gives Congress authority to legislate with respect to taxation, interstate commerce, and the property owned by the United States. However, the federal government has no general authority to regulate human conduct for public health and safety. This power is called the police power. Under the Tenth Amendment all powers that are not specifically given to the federal government are reserved to the states, so it is the states which have retained the "police power." Under the rubric of police power, states may enact laws necessary for the protection and promotion of public health, safety and welfare.

If a community comprehensive plan is to achieve its purpose, it must be implemented in part by legal controls upon the use of private land. These land use controls are based on the state's police power. A municipal corporation is a political subdivision of the state but it has no inherent police power. Municipalities possess only those powers granted them by the state constitution or statutes. Therefore, if a municipality is to exert public controls over private property, it must be given that power in enabling legislation. All states have enabling legislation granting to municipalities the power to control land uses. When a municipality exceeds this authority its actions are termed *ultra vires,* or outside the scope of authority.

Beyond the authorization issue, the basic tests for the constitutional validity of land use regulations are few in number and can be reduced to three propositions:

1. restrictions on land use must promote the public health, safety, morals, and welfare;
2. such restrictions must not be arbitrary and capricious; and
3. such restrictions must be reasonable to the extent that a landowner must have a reasonable opportunity to use the property and not experience a substantial loss of value.

These criteria are applied by the courts on a case by case basis. Beyond the legal authorization and constitutional limitations, there are few legal constraints on the exercise of police power by states and municipalities.

Zoning. Zoning is the principal tool employed to implement the comprehensive plan. State enabling legislation typically requires that the zoning ordinance be based on a comprehensive plan, although the general view is that the plan and the ordinance are separate and autonomous documents. The blueprint for most state zoning legislation is a model act prepared in the 1920's by the U.S. Department of Commerce, titled the Standard Zoning Enabling Act.[13] This Act outlines a diversity of controls by providing that municipalities have the power to:

> regulate and restrict the height, number of stories, and size of buildings and other structures, the percentage of a lot that may be occupied, the size of yards, courts, and other open spaces, the density of population, and the location and use of buildings, structures and land for trade, industry, residence and other purposes.[14]

All of these regulatory provisions can be found in the lexicon of zoning and in the ordinances of most municipalities. Zoning, however, is not the sole instrument for controlling land use and contains numerous shortcomings. The typical zoning ordinance provides no guide to the planning of new streets and utility corridors; it contains only minimum standards for platting of new neighborhoods; it offers no guarantee that open space will be preserved, and it offers no protection from financial losses to the community from improper development. These protections are provided by subdivision controls.

Subdivision Controls. Regulation of the development process through subdivision controls is second only to zoning as a primary land use control method. Whereas zoning controls the uses of land before, during, and after development, subdivision controls apply primarily to the development process and once land is subdivided, subdivision controls have limited application. In land development, the subdivision process pertains to the division of a lot, tract, or parcel of land into two or more smaller lots. The general purpose of subdivision control is to regulate this process, thereby promoting the orderly physical and economic growth of undeveloped areas within a municipality.

The need for subdivision development control became apparent in the land boom of the 1920's. Land developers were more interested in a quick profit than in creating well planned subdivisions. Cities, eagerly seeking expansion, installed improvements before lots were sold, with the expectation that future purchasers would pay for the costs by special assessments. But often lots were not sold, or the assessments were so high that tax delinquencies resulted. As a result, cities in the 1930's and 1940's had subdivisions with millions of vacant platted lots and an inadequate tax base to support services to these areas. The burden eventually was shifted to the general taxpayer.[15] Reacting to this abuse, many states enacted statutes granting municipalities the authority to control the subdivision of land. Municipalities had come to realize that new subdivisions needed to be better integrated into plans for future development and the provision of public services. Today all states have enacted some form of subdivision control regulations.[16]

Building Codes. Municipalities are empowered by state law, under the broad rubric of police power, to enact building and housing codes. Building codes set standards regulating the material which may be used in construction, as well as the manner in which the building itself must be constructed. The purpose of a building code is to insure that the structure is safe for occupancy. Housing codes set minimum standards for the occupancy of residential units. Items covered in such codes typically include water, heating, utility, space and ventilation requirements. The major purpose of the housing code is to regulate the living conditions of residential units to prevent blight and overcrowding.[17]

While building and housing codes do not directly regulate land uses, they are the basic instrument used by municipalities to secure compliance with zoning regulations.[18] Typically a building permit will not be issued unless there is compliance with the building code and the zoning ordinance. This may require approval by the zoning administrator and building official. While the building permit is used to detect compliance with the zoning ordinance, municipalities have, through the issuance of a "certificate of occupancy," a further control device to insure zoning compliance. To insure that no building can be used which does not comply with the zoning ordinance, an inspection is made after building completion, but before use. If this inspection reveals compliance, a "certificate of occupancy" is issued. No building can be used unless this certificate has been issued.

Environmental Permits. Federal, state and local governments have adopted a number of regulatory programs for the protection of environmental areas and resources. Unlike zoning, environmental land use regulation is characterized by federal and state intervention. Federal control over wetlands and floodplains is derived from the Clean Water Act and the flood insurance program.[19] Many states have also enacted regulatory programs to protect specific environmental resources such as shorelands, wetlands, natural rivers and floodplains. Although these regulatory schemes may not include zoning, by incorporating permit conditions the final result is land use control. Many of these state regulatory programs preempt local regulation. Whether a local regulation is preempted is often determined by the language of the specific state regulatory legislation.

Transfer of Development Rights. The legal basis underlying this approach recognizes that title to property is composed of a "bundle of individual rights," any of which may be severed from the rest and transferred to another. Thus, mineral rights to property may be separated from the surface estate and sold apart from surface rights. One of the components of this "bundle of rights" is the right to develop the land. This development right is a component of great value among the many rights of ownership.

Transfer of development rights (TDR) has been used to protect historic sites, open space, and agricultural land. A TDR program allows the owner of a historic building, precluded from demolishing the structure and constructing a high rise building, to transfer the development rights to another landowner or site. The purchaser of this right pays the owner of the historic site for the unused development rights. TDR can be a useful land use control, but apart from a few states and municipalities, it represents an idea whose time has not yet come.[20]

C. SUBDIVISION CONTROL PROCESS

The general power of a municipality to exercise control over development of land subdivisions within and outside its boundaries is derived from state planning and land platting statutes. It has been universally recognized that subdividing land is a privilege to which the municipality may attach reasonable conditions. If a developer fails to meet these conditions, the land cannot be subdivided and lots sold. Modern subdivision ordinances have evolved from simple platting requirements which imposed few burdens on the developer to a range of mandated requirements. The purposes of today's subdivision controls can be categorized into four general areas:

1. to regulate the division of land into smaller parcels;
2. to simplify the recording of land and to aid in conveying clean titles to purchasers;
3. to supervise and control the layout of public features such as streets, utility corridors, water and sewer lines, drainage ways, schools sites and park and recreation areas; and
4. to transfer the costs of these public facilities from the city to the developer and ultimately to the buyers of the newly developed land.

These regulations benefit the municipality, the developers and the lot purchasers in that the city is assured of orderly development, developers have standards as guides and purchasers have a well-planned subdivision.

Enabling legislation and local subdivision ordinances vary as to which municipal agency should have primary approval authority. The most prevalent practice is to vest this authority in a municipal planning commission and to allow the commission to promulgate rules governing not only the plat approval process, but also the imposition of conditions as a prerequisite to approval. (The legal authority and reasonableness of these preconditions is the subject of Chapter Three.) Municipalities are often granted authority to control subdivision development for prescribed distances beyond their borders.[21] The courts have generally affirmed the right of the legislature to grant this extraterritorial plat approval jurisdiction to municipalities. In rural areas, counties or regional agencies may have plat approval authority.

Plat review procedures vary according to the size of the community, the level of development activity and the complexity of the ordinance. Generally, the plat review process is either two tier, for minor subdivisions (sketch plat, and final plat) or three tier, for major subdivisions (sketch, preliminary and final plat).[22] The definition of minor and major is either set forth in state statute or defined in the local ordinance.

When park land dedication is required, the land should be selected at the sketch plat stage. The ordinance should state when the final dedication is to be perfected, which is usually at the time of approval of the final plat. Thus, the jurisdiction must decide on land or fee or both, and when and how any fee is to be paid.

As part of the plat review procedure the park and recreation officials and the planners should inspect the plat and proposed park site and adjacent lands prior to making a final recommendation on land, fee or both. At the time of final plat approval the developers should be required to furnish all covenants for private open space and recreation facilities, the perpetual management contract, and the development schedule for the park(s), these should all have been previously reviewed and approved by legal counsel for the jurisdiction. (See Figure 2.2)

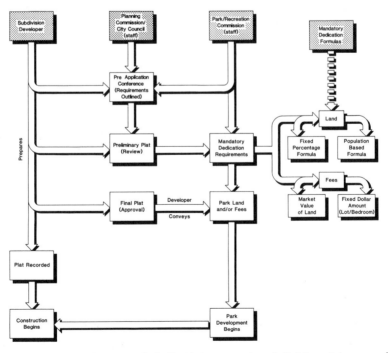

Figure 2-2 The mandatory park dedication process in subdivision plat approval.

§2.4. Preapplication Phase

This phase gives the developer an opportunity to confer with city staff regarding plat approval conditions before formal application is made. A developer typically prepares a preliminary plat sketch delineating lots in relationship to existing and proposed community facilities. (See Figure 2-3). Planning staff review this sketch to determine if it conforms to the master plan and to city design and construction standards. With the advent of modern subdivision control legislation, there is a close relationship between a comprehensive plan and subdivision approval. In the majority of jurisdictions, the subdivision plat must conform to the official map or master plan. Failure to conform is a basis for rejection of the subdivision plat. Reference should be made to the enabling legislation and case law in each state for the connection between the master plan and the subdivision rejection.

In the preapplication phase, planning staff may suggest plat improvements, and provide developers with standards by which the plat is reviewed and approved. The authority of the city to promulgate and impose these precondition standards is the basis for mandatory dedication of park land and open space. In addition to park land standards the majority of states incorporate these additional standards as conditions for plat approval:

1. that the streets be of sufficient width, grade and location to afford adequate access and that they be in conformance with the official street plan;
2. that the lots on the plat be of such character and dimension that they can be used safely for building purposes;
3. that legal monuments and parks be described so as to facilitate proper surveying and legal description;
4. that all streets, sidewalks, water and sewer lines, storm drains and utility easements be designed in accordance with local building codes and standards; and
5. that the plat show, if so required by the subdivision ordinance, a park or parks of reasonable size for recreation purposes as specified in the park and recreation master plan.[23]

The developer's preliminary plat of the subdivision must conform to the required standards.

§2.5. Preliminary Plat Approval

After agreement has been reached during the preapplication phase, the developer prepares a preliminary plat and supporting data for consideration by the planning commission. A preliminary plat is a map of the area, drawn

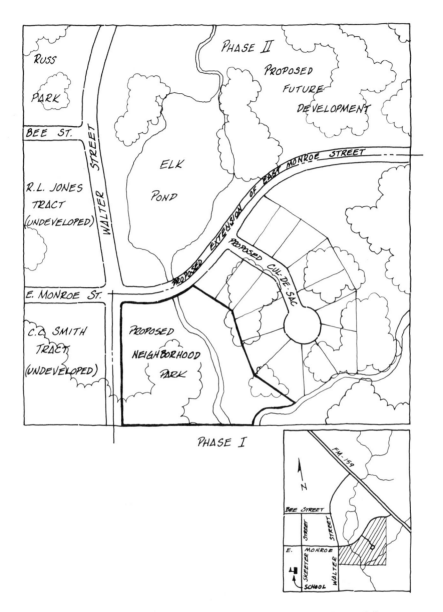

Figure 2-3 A proposed subdivision sketch plat with park location and future development.

to scale, depicting the lots, streets, utility corridors and parks, if required.[24] (See Figure 2-4). Before the hearing by the planning commission, city staff reviews the plat for compliance with the master plan and design standards.

After the hearing, the planning commission may recommend plat approval, attach additional conditions before final approval, or reject the preliminary plat.

§2.6. Final Plat Approval

After the preliminary plat is approved the developer prepares a final plat and submits it for approval by the planning commission and city council. The final plat must substantially conform to the preliminary plat and contain all necessary information for recording. (See Figure 2-5). A final plat is not official until the developer delivers the necessary copies to the clerk of the specified agency for recording. Once the plat is recorded, lots can be sold and housing construction started.

D. DETERMINING PARK DEDICATION REQUIREMENTS

It is well established that other standards and conditions set out in enabling legislation and local regulations may be imposed on the developer in connection with approval of a subdivision plat. Standards may require the dedication of land for streets, highways, utilities, drainage systems and parks. Authority for such control is derived from state enabling legislation, so conditions may be imposed only if authorized by a state statute. The right to impose certain exactions on developers as a condition of plat approval is grounded upon a dual premise. First, the health, safety and welfare of the residents of the proposed subdivision with respect to streets, sewer, water and utilities is a paramount consideration justifying the exercise of the police power. Second, public policy dictates that developers assist municipalities in constructing public improvements since they will be the initial beneficiaries of the development. The conditions of approval which the city imposes on the developer for whatever public policy reason must be reasonable. Unreasonable conditions attached to the approval will be invalidated by the courts.

Historically, there is established precedent for the required dedication of streets, sewers, water drainage and utility easements.[25] More recently, many states have expanded the list of conditions to include parks, recreation areas, open space and school sites. The legality of this approach is covered in Chapter Three; it generally depends on whether there is enabling legislation to impose the conditions, whether the local ordinance authorizes the conditions, and whether the conditions are reasonable.

Municipalities use various formulas to determine the amount of land to be dedicated or fees in lieu of land to be charged. (See Figure 2-2) The

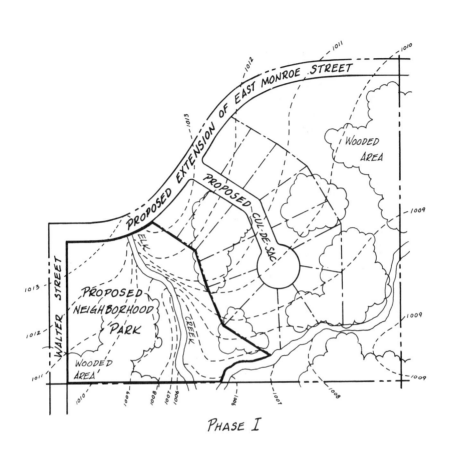

PHASE I

VICINITY MAP

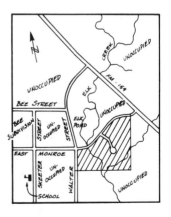

Figure 2-4 A preliminary subdivision plat.

amount of park land required to meet the needs of a neighborhood may be based on several factors including the geographic size of the neighborhood, the projected population density, the proximity of other parks and the classification of neighborhood parks. Park planning and space standards come into play when determining neighborhood park acreage needs. All of these factors must be taken into account when developing the acreage requirements in the mandatory park land dedication ordinance.

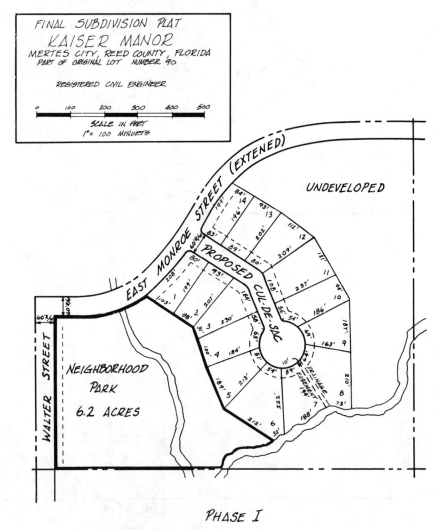

FINAL SUBDIVISION PLAT
KAISER MANOR
MERTES CITY, REED COUNTY, FLORIDA
PART OF ORIGINAL LOT NUMBER 90

REGISTERED CIVIL ENGINEER

SCALE IN FEET
1"= 100 MINUETS

PHASE I

Figure 2-5 A final subdivision plat.

22

§2.7. Acreage Formulas

There are two principal formulas for determining the basis and the amount of land to be dedicated in subdivision ordinances: (1) a fixed percentage based on the total amount of land in the subdivision and (2) a population formula based on the density or number of dwelling units in the subdivision.[26] Under either approach, the formulas must be reasonable and related to park and recreation space standards.

In a survey of cities that require open space dedication by some method, the most common formula used was the fixed percentage.[27] A typical fixed percentage subdivision ordinance might read:

> a minimum of 10 percent of the net area of major subdivisions of more than 50 lots, or 25 acres, shall be dedicated for public parks or playgrounds.

This formula is based on the size of the subdivision and is intended to apply to major subdivisions. For a 25-acre development, a minimum of 2.5 acres would have to be dedicated. The major disadvantage of the fixed percentage formula is that it does not take into account the density of the residential development. The standard remains the same whether the subdivision is a single family development or a multiple family complex, although the needs generated by the two will obviously be different. It is often argued that this formula ignores the planning principles relating site needs to population densities for the sake of simplicity and ease of administration.

Relating park needs to the number of people in a geographical area is the major advantage of the population based approach. Land requirements can be calculated on either (1) the density of the subdivision or (2) the number of dwelling units in the subdivision.

§2.8. Fees in Lieu of Land

Not all land in a subdivision is suited for park development purposes. The ordinance should therefore allow the community to accept cash as a substitute for the land. If a cash fee is required the fee should be based on a formula that reflects the fair market value of the land not dedicated within the subdivision, or of land in proximity to the subdivision service area. The cash should be deposited in a special fund and used only for land acquisition or facility development benefiting the residents from whom the fee was generated.

E. MERITS OF PARK DEDICATION

Persuasive pro and con arguments can be advanced regarding mandatory dedication of park land as a condition for securing plat approval.[28] The primary parties involved are the local government representatives, the land developers, and the citizens of the community.

Local Government

Pros

1. Assures that local park and open space requirements are met at the time an area is platted and that local government will not have to pay an exorbitant price for land which was either reserved or "set aside" by the developer.

2. Allows for the joint location of park and school sites.

3. Allows the selection of appropriate park locations at the time streets are being laid out.

4. Protects the community from overly inflated land costs.

5. Encourages more efficient land development strategies such as clustering, or planned community developments.

6. Creates future value for the community in the same manner as other appropriate land development controls.

Cons

1. Adds to the cost of development which will be transferred to the lot purchasers, although they will be the principal beneficiaries of the regulation. Over the time of a normal mortgage this cost is minimal and is offset by the appreciative value enhancement impact of public facilities such as parks which people consider an essential element in a desirable neighborhood.

2. Causes the community to expend funds to develop and maintain the park prior to the full ripening of the tax base of the subdivision.

3. Communities with mandatory dedication ordinances may tend to utilize this technique as the only method of acquiring additional park land and relax standard techniques.

Developer

Pros

1. Makes available strategically located neighborhood parks which enhance the saleability of the property.

2. Allows otherwise non-developable land to be effectively utilized as part of the park.

3. Allows, in some cases, land dedicated for public park purposes to be deducted from local real estate taxes.

4. Lowers basic development costs when utilizing clustering and other innovative development techniques.

5. Provides, where available through local ordinances, density bonus incentives for generous dedications.

Cons

1. Lowers the total number of lots that may be developed.

2. Increases the cost of subdividing, which may not be fully recouped from increased lot prices.

Resident

Pros

1. Allows immediate development of park land when the resident moves in, as opposed to waiting, often five to ten years for the park to be developed (if the land is there for development).

2. Avoids overcrowding of existing parks.

3. Adds diversity, character and environmental integrity to the neighborhood.

4. Increases property values of homes adjacent to or close to parks and open space lands.

Cons

1. Leads to higher property taxes in order to support the governmental expenditures for the park.

2. In some cases undevelopable land may not be desirable for park use because of terrain, location, physical barriers and limited access.

F. SUMMARY

As growth and land use conflicts intensify, land use planning and its companion land use controls will increase in complexity. Within this complex web of regulations, the concept of acquiring park land through mandatory subdivision exactions has evolved. This chapter has outlined the relationship between planning, land use regulations and mandatory dedication of park land.

Any planner will tell you that comprehensive planning comes first. Municipalities adopt and administer land use regulations in order to implement the comprehensive plan. Any land use lawyer will tell you that courts have not universally accepted the "planning first" rule. The majority holds that the "in accordance" requirement of state enabling legislation does not require a municipality to prepare and adopt a plan prior to exercising the zoning power.[29] In adopting this rule the courts have adopted a narrow interpretation of planning legislation by not requiring planning prior to enforcement. A related planning issue is whether the land use regulations must be "consistent" with the comprehensive plan. In reviewing "consistency issues" the courts have adopted a "rule of reason" when determining whether zoning classifications conform with comprehensive plan classification. If the zoning classification is reasonably related to the plan classification, courts will require "consistency." This rule is generally followed in those states which require comprehensive planning and that require land use regulations to be consistent with the plan.

Municipalities are not sovereign and may only exercise those powers granted by the state. All states have delegated to municipalities the powers of taxation, eminent domain and land use regulation. While the police power is the basis for most land use controls, taxation and eminent domain are also used to regulate land development. Tax programs can affect the land development process but only through economic incentives or disincentives. Because taxation operates on a large scale, it is not effective as a site specific control. Eminent domain provides limited opportunities as a city wide land use control; it operates best at a site specific level, for example, in purchasing of property for a park. Nevertheless, under the powers of taxation and eminent domain municipalities can regulate the land development process.

Police powers provide the legal basis for exercising the basic body of land use regulations. Municipalities enact the majority of land use controls under their police power. Specific regulations include zoning, environmental controls and subdivision regulations. Local subdivision regulation is authorized by state enabling legislation. While subdivision ordinances contain requirements for design and standards for construction, they may also require land dedications from developers for streets, highways, utility corridors and parks. This forms the basis for acquisition of neighborhood park land through mandatory dedication.

CHAPTER TWO NOTES

1. Fred Bossleman, *The Quiet Revolution in Land Use Controls,* The Council on Environmental Quality (Washington, D.C.: U.S. Gov't. Printing Office 1971).
2. See Robert Frielich, *Awakening the Sleeping Giant: New Trends and Developments in Environmental Land Use Controls,* 1974 Institute on Planning, Zoning and Eminent Domain 1, 2-3, (Dallas: S.W. Legal Foundation, 1974).
3. Donald Hagman, *Urban Planning and Land Development Control Law* (St. Paul, Minn: West Publishing Co., 1971), pp. 38-39.
4. See Anderson and Roswig, Planning, Zoning, Subdivisions: A Summary of Statutory Law in the 50 States, Chart 9, p. 212 (1966).
5. *Forks Township Board v. G. Calantoni and Sons, Inc.,* 297 A.2d 164 (1972).
6. Delogu, *Taxing Power as a Land Use Control Device,* 45 Denver L.J. 279 (1968).
7. McQuillan Municipal Corp., (3rd ed.) §32.06.
8. Hagman, *Urban Planning,* Supra, p. 365.
9. Alexandra Dawson, *Land Use Planning and the Law,* (New York: Garland St. Pen Press, 1982), p. 130.
10. Keene, *Differential Assessment and the Preservation of Open Space,* 14 Urban Law Annual 11 (1977).
11. 26 Am Jur 2d, Eminent Domain, §1.
12. Ibid, §2.
13. U.S. Dept. of Commerce, Standard Zoning Enabling Act (U.S. Gov't. Printing Office: Wash. D.C. 1926).
14. Ibid, 2.
15. See Hagman, *Urban Planning,* Supra, pp 245-259.
16. See Appendix B for a listing of state legislation.
17. Edmund Vitale, *Building Regulations* (New York: Charles Scribners' Sons, 1979), pp 12-15.
18. Robert Anderson, *American Law of Zoning 2nd,* §17.02, p. 88.
19. 33 USCA §1344.
20. For a discussion of the concept see Jerome Rose, *The Transfer of Development Rights: a New Technique of Land Use Regulation* (New Brunswick, New Jersey; Center for Urban Policy @ Rutgers, 1975).
21. In Illinois for example this distance is 1 1/2 miles, Ill. Rev. Stat, 1979, Ch. 115, par. 13.
22. Rohan, *Zoning and Land Use Controls* (New York: Matthew Bender, 1985) Subdivision Controls, §45.02.
23. Rothkopf, *The Law of Planning and Zoning* (NY: Clark Boardman Co., LTD, 1984) 71-16-18.
24. Blacks Law Dictionary 4th ed., p. 1309.
25. Heyman and Gilhool, *The Constitutionality of Imposing Increased Community Costs on New Suburban Residents through Subdivision Exactions,* 73 Yale L.J. 1119 (1964).
26. See Mary Brooks, "Mandatory Dedication of Land or Fees in Lieu of Land for Parks and Schools," American Society of Planning Officials Report No. 266, February 1971, for a technical guide.
27. International City Management Association, *1969 Municipal Yearbook* (Washing-

ton, DC: ICMA, 1969), p. 237.

28. This discussion is taken from an article by Bruce Kramer and James Mertes, Securing Parkland Through Mandatory Dedication, *Texas Recreation and Parks Society,* April/May 1979, pp. 20-26.

29. *Kozesnik v. Montgomery,* 131A.2d 1 (NJ 1957); *Furtney v. Simsbury Zoning Commission,* 271 A.2d 319 (Conn. 1970); *Dawson Enterprises, Inc. v. Blaine County,* 567 P.2d 1257 (Idaho 1977); *Nottingham Village, Inc. v. Baltimore County,* 292 A.2d 680 (Md. 1972); *Allred v. City of Raleigh,* 173 S.E.2d 533 (N.C. App. 1970), rev'd on other grounds, 178 S.E.2d 432 (1971); *Udell v. Haas,* 235 N.E.2d 897 (N.Y. 1968); *Cleaver v. Board of Adjustment,* 200 A.2d 408 (Pa. 1964); *Hadley v. Harold Realty Co.,* 198 A.2d 149 (R.I. 1964); *West Hall Citizens for Controlled Dev. Density v. King County Council,* 627 P.2d 1002 (Wash. App. 1981).

CHAPTER THREE

Legal Issues in Park Land Dedication

This chapter will be devoted to a discussion of the legal issues associated with mandatory dedication of park land. The cases addressing the validity of mandatory dedication provisions generally agree on two points. First, there must be valid statutory enabling authority before a municipality may impose these requirements as part of subdivision plat approval. Second, the exercise of the power to impose the park land dedication requirement must not violate Federal and State constitutional protections.

A. LEGAL AUTHORIZATION

Litigation challenging the authority of the state, acting through municipalities, to regulate subdivision development is rare. Subdivision controls and exactions were upheld at an early date and their general validity has been consistently affirmed.[1] Statutes relating to the platting of lands can be found very early in state legislation. As far back as 1833 and 1839 such statutes were to be found in the Laws of Michigan and in the Revised Statutes of Wisconsin.[2] As an exercise of the police power, subdivision controls can be sustained if they are "reasonable." In the context of mandatory park land dedication three (3) court tests have been used to gauge "reasonableness"; these will be discussed in section B of this chapter.

As creatures of the state, municipalities have only those powers expressly granted by the state constitution and enabling legislation. Municipal authority to regulate the subdivision of land and impose conditions for the dedication of parks is derived from home rule, general planning, or subdivision control legislation. All states have delegated to municipalities authority to impose subdivision controls. (See Appendix B for a compilation of statutes). While state enabling acts vary in specific details, the models for modern subdivision controls are The Standard City Planning Enabling Act, Model Municipal Planning Act, and the Model Subdivision Regulation Act.[3] Provisions from these model acts can be found in most state statutes.

At the municipal level, subdivision control is implemented by the subdivision control ordinance and the rules and regulations of the planning commission. In regulating subdivision development, municipalities must strictly conform with the substantive and procedural dictates of the enabling statute and may not expand upon specific statutory authorizations.

§3.1. Home Rule

Home rule refers to a right of self-government granted to municipalities under provisions of a state constitution or legislation. These home rule powers are exercised through the adoption of a municipal charter. Once adopted, the charter becomes the organic law of the municipality, having all the force of an act of the state legislature.[4] Home rule cities have all the powers of self-government and look to the acts of the legislature not for grants of power but for limitations on their power. Consequently, when a city charter authorizes subdivision regulations no separate enabling legislation is needed to impose the regulations. The Charter of Cincinnati, Ohio, for example, provides:

> All plats of the subdivision of land within the corporate limits of the city ***
> and all instruments of dedication of land for public use shall be submitted to
> the commission and approved *** before they may be offered for record.[5]

A recent case regarding the authority of home rule cities to impose park land dedication requirements pursuant to a city charter provision is *City of College Station v. Turtle Rock Corp.*, 680 S.W.2d 802 (Tx 1984). The City of College Station, a home rule city, enacted a park land dedication ordinance requiring, *inter alia* that a developer grant to the city a fee simple dedication of 1 acre of land for each 133 proposed dwelling units. The developer challenged this requirement, claiming that the enabling statutes limited the authority of Texas cities to acquiring land by negotiated purchase. The court stated that the purpose of the enabling statutes was to grant powers to cities. Hence the park land dedication ordinance was upheld.

Other jurisdictions that have recognized the authority of home rule cities to impose mandatory park land dedication, or fees in-lieu thereof, without specific state enabling acts are:

California.	*Hirsch v. City of Mountain View,* 134 Cal Rptr 519 (1976), *Ayers v. City Council of City of Los Angeles,* 207 P.2d 1 (1949);
Colorado.	*Bethlehem Evangelical Luthern Church v. City of Lakewood,* 626 P.2d 668 (1981);

| Florida. | *Hollywood Inc. v. Broward Co.*, 431 So.2d 606 (1983); |
| Wyoming. | *Coulter v. City of Rawlings*, 662 P.2d 888 (1983). |

Some jurisdictions have not recognized the dedication authority of home rule cities. In *Admiral Development Corp. v. City of Maitland,* 267 So.2d 860 (Fla 1972), the Florida Supreme Court ruled that the park land dedication ordinance was beyond the scope of the city's authority under its charter and even if it were authorized by charter the language of the ordinance was so overbroad as to render it invalid. In *Maitland,* the city's ordinance required that at least five percent of the gross area of lands to be subdivided within the city be dedicated to the city for parks. The Florida court acknowledged that the power to impose dedication requirements may come from a city charter but concluded that the charter did not include express or implied provisions authorizing the establishment of park land dedication conditions.

§3.2. Enabling Legislation

A municipality's power to impose a park land dedication or a fee-in-lieu requirement is rarely made explicit in state legislation.[6] Exceptions to this are in the states of California, Connecticut, Hawaii, Minnesota, Montana, Nevada, New York, North Carolina and Vermont, whose enabling acts specifically authorize mandatory park dedications as a precondition to subdivision approval. (See Appendix B.)

In the absence of an express delegation of power the majority of the courts have implied that authority from a broad interpretation of planning, zoning, subdivision control or land acquisition enabling legislation. This is illustrated in *Call v. City of West Jordan,* 606 P.2d 217 (Utah 1979), where the court acknowledged that "it is impractical for statutes to spell out to the last detail of all the things city governments must do to perform the functions imposed upon them by law." In *Call,* the state statute did not specifically authorize the city to require a dedication of seven percent of the land area of a proposed subdivision. Nonetheless, the Utah Supreme Court implied the authority from the city's responsibility to have a planning commission and to adopt a master plan.

Courts in other jurisdictions have addressed the issue of implied statutory authority for park land dedication ordinances. The majority of decisions have upheld the implied power of municipalities to require dedication or fees in lieu thereof.[7] In *Jordan v. Village of Menomonee Falls,* 137 N.W.2d 442 (Wisc 1965), for example, the court reasoned that the statute authorizing the formation of a planning commission also was designed to facilitate the development of parks; therefore, the city was empowered to mandate that subdi-

viders dedicate property for park purposes. The *Jordan* court also decided
that the fee charged in-lieu of actual land dedication was not a tax but rather a
charge imposed in the plat approval process. The Jordan holding was followed in *Brookhill Development Ltd. v. City of Waukesha*, 299 N.W.2d 610
(Wisc 1980), where the court upheld an ordinance requiring dedication of
land for school purposes.

Recognizing that municipal powers are not necessarily limited to those
expressly conferred, other courts have followed the general rule of law that
powers may be implied from the statutes. The following states have followed
this broad interpretation in upholding municipal park land dedication ordinances.

Colorado.	*Bethlehem Evangelical Luthern Church v. City of Lakewood,* 626 P.2d 668 (1981).
Connecticut.	*Aunt Hack Ridge Estates, Inc. v. City of Danbury,* 273 A.2d 880 (1970).
Florida.	*Hollywood Inc. v. Broward Co.* 431 So.2d 606 (1983), *Broward Co. v. Janis Development Corp.* 311 So.2d 371 (1975).
Illinois.	*Board of Education of DuPage Co. v. Surety Developers, Inc.,* 347 N.E.2d 149 (1976).
Minnesota.	*Collis v. City of Bloomington,* 246 S.W.2d 19 (1976).
Missouri.	*Home Builders Assoc. of Greater Kansas City v. City of Kansas City,* 555 S.W.2d 832 (1977).
Montana.	*Billings Properties Inc. v. Yellowstone Co.,* 394 P.2d 188 (1964).
Nevada.	*Crucil v. Carson City,* 600 P.2d 216 (1979).
New Hampshire.	*Patenaude v. Town of Meredith,* 392 A.2d 582 (1978).
New York.	*Jenad, Inc. v. Village of Scarsdale,* 218 N.E.2d 673 (1966).
North Carolina.	*Messer v. Town of Chapel Hill,* 297 S.E.2d 632 (1982).
Rhode Island.	*Ansuini v. City of Cranston,* 264 A.2d 910 (1970).
Texas.	*City of College Station v. Turtle Rock Corp,* 680 S.W.2d 802 (1984).
Utah.	*Call v. City of West Jordan,* 606 P.2d 217 (1980).
Washington.	*Hillis Homes Inc. v. Snohomish Co.,* 650 P.2d 193 (1982).
Wisconsin.	*Jordan v. Village of Menomonee Falls,* 137 N.W.2d 442 (1965).
Wyoming.	*Coulter v. City of Rawlins,* 662 P.2d 888 (1983).

Not all courts follow the implied authority rule. In most of these cases,
the critical issue was the fee-in-lieu-of-land requirement. Generally, courts

rejecting the implied authority argument have strictly interpreted the cash fees to be taxes. Illustrative of this line of reasoning is *Coronado Development Co. v. City of McPherson*, 368 P.2d 51 (Kan 1962). In that case the court upheld the land exactions but struck down the fee-in-lieu requirement.

Still other courts have used a restrictive statutory interpretation, invalidating park land dedication ordinances on the grounds that the power was not specifically enunciated in the statute. These jurisdictions follow the narrow interpretation rule.

Alabama.	*City of Montgomery v. Crossroads Land Co.*, 355 So.2d 363 (1978).
Kansas.	*Coronado Development Co. v. City of McPherson*, 368 P.2d 51 (1962).
Michigan.	*Ridgemont Development Co. v. City of East Detroit*, 100 N.W.2d 301 (1960).
New Jersey.	*West Park Ave. v. Township of Ocean*, 224 A.2d 1 (1966).
New Mexico.	*Sanchez v. City of Santa Fe*, 481 P.2d 401 (1971).
Oregon.	*Haugen v. Gleason*, 359 P.2d 108 (1961).

Several states have adopted statutes specifically authorizing dedications or fees in lieu for park and school sites. This approach was tested in the frequently cited case of *Associated Homebuilders of Greater East Bay, Inc. v. City of Walnut Creek*, 484 P.2d 606 (Calif 1971), appeal dismissed 404 U.S. 878 (U.S. Sup.Ct. 1971). The California Supreme Court upheld the statute authorizing land dedications and in-lieu fees for park and recreation purposes. It is noteworthy that the court went beyond earlier tests to suggest that the statute could "be justified on the basis of general public need for recreational facilities caused by present and future subdivisions." States that have specific statutory authority for park land dedication include:

California.	Calif. Gov. Code, §66477;
Connecticut.	Gen. Stat. of Conn. §8-26;
Hawaii.	Haw. Rev. Stat. §46-6;
Minnesota.	Minn. Stat. Ann. §462-358;
Montana.	Mont. Code Ann. §76-3-606;
New York.	N.Y. Gen. Mun. Laws. 277, §7-730;
North Carolina.	Gen. Stat. of N.C. §160A-372;
Vermont.	Ver. Stat. Ann. §4417.

Many court decisions recognize that it is impractical for a state legislature to spell out to the last detail all of the things city governments must do to perform the functions imposed on them by law. The majority of the courts, in the absence of an express delegation of mandatory dedication powers in a state enabling act, have implied the necessary authority from planning and subdivision control legislation. However, when a municipality imposes a fee-in-lieu-of-land requirement the courts have taken a more conservative approach and have invalidated a number of ordinances.

B. CONSTITUTIONAL ISSUES

The use of mandatory park land dedication is advantageous to municipalities because it allows them to acquire land without using public revenues; it places the cost on the developer whose subdividing activities have generated the demand for the services.[8] This practice has generated significant state litigation on whether mandatory dedication constitutes a taking of private property for public use for which just compensation is required or whether the practice is merely a regulation for which no compensation is required. Although the constitutionality of this practice can be challenged in federal or state courts, the federal courts have deferred jurisdiction to the state courts. This deferral is probably because most state statutes allow an appeal from a municipal decision to a state trial court and because federal courts abstain from acting on predominantly state land use issues.[9] Since the United States Supreme Court has found the federal constitutional challenge to be without merit, the relevant case law is derived from state courts.[10]

Although the majority of state courts agree on the need for park land generated by a developer's activity, they disagree on how to measure the "reasonableness" of the method through which a municipality specifies how much land should be dedicated. Three somewhat different tests have been developed by the courts to measure the "reasonableness" of the mandatory park land exactions. Each of these tests, the "Specifically and Uniquely Attributable Test," the "Rational Nexus Test" and the "Reasonably Related Test" can be traced to a particular court case. These tests have been extensively reviewed, analyzed and criticized by legal commentators in reviewing park land dedication practices. (See Appendix F for a listing of Law Reviews.)

§3.3. Specifically and Uniquely Attributable Test

The most restrictive of the three tests was developed by the Illinois Supreme Court in *Pioneer Trust and Savings Bank v. Village of Mount Prospect,* 176 N.E.2d 799 (1961). The Illinois court, in reviewing the reasonableness of an ordinance requiring developers to dedicate one acre of park land per sixty families, articulated the following test for distinguishing taking and valid exercise of the police power:

> **If the requirement is within the statutory grant of power to the municipality and if the burden cast upon the subdivider is specifically and uniquely attributable to his activity, then the requirement is permissible; if not, it is forbidden and amounts to a confiscation of private property*** (176 N.E.2d 801).

The court then applied this test to invalidate the particular park land dedication ordinance. Subsequently, in *Krughoff v. City of Naperville,* 369 N.E.2d 892, (Ill 1977) the Illinois court reaffirmed *Pioneer Trust* but relaxed its scrutiny over how strictly the city was to show its need for the facility.

Commentators have criticized *Pioneer Trust* as creating an unduly restrictive and unworkable standard for testing the validity of park land dedications.[11] This approach is unworkable, particularly in smaller subdivisions. For example, how would a thirty-lot subdivision provide half a baseball diamond or tennis court?[12] A key aspect of the *Pioneer Trust* test is that the burden of proof of ordinance validity rests on the city. This is contrary to the view in the other two tests, which presume the ordinance is valid. Recognizing that it is often impossible for a municipality to prove that the need for the park was generated "solely" by the increase in population of the new subdivision, many state courts have cited with approval *Pioneer Trust* but have followed a more lenient approach. The "specifically and uniquely attributable" test was cited and apparently approved by the Montana Supreme Court in *Billings Properties, Inc. v. Yellowstone County,* 394 P.2d 182 (Mont 1964), but this case was distinguished from *Pioneer Trust* on the ground that the legislature had determined by statute in Montana that subdivisions of a certain size needed parks. This obvious deference to the legislature is inconsistent with the process of scrutiny of dedications contemplated in *Pioneer Trust.*

Despite the restrictive nature of the test and the fact that the municipality has the burden of demonstrating the need for the park, a minority of jurisdictions apply the "specifically and uniquely attributable" test. These states have court decisions directly using that test.

Connecticut.	*Aunt Hack Ridge Estates, Inc. v. City of Danbury,* 273 A.2d 890 (1970).
Florida.	*Admiral Development Corp. v. City of Maitland,* 267 So.2d 863 (1976).
New Hampshire.	*J.E.D. Assoc. Inc. v. Town of Atkinson,* 432 A.2d 12 (1981).
Ohio.	*McKain v. Toledo City Plan. Comm'n.,* 270 N.E.2d 370 (1971).

Rhode Island. *Frank Ansuini Inc. v. City of Cranston,* 264 A.2d 910 (1970).

§3.4. Rational Nexus Test

After *Pioneer Trust* many courts began moving away from that standard, while still accepting the premise upon which the theory was predicated. An intermediate standard—the rational nexus test—evolved. In 1965 the Wisconsin Supreme Court in *Jordan v. Village of Menomonee Falls,* 137 N.W.2d 442, appeal dismissed, 385 U.S. 4 (1966), accepted the *Pioneer Trust* test in principle but modified it in application. The court adopted the following refinement:

> We deem this [the "specifically and uniquely attributable" test] to be an acceptable statement of the yardstick to be applied, provided the word 'specifically and uniquely attributable to his activity' are not so restrictively applied as to cast an unreasonable burden of proof upon the municipality which has enacted the ordinance under attack. In most instances it would be impossible for the municipality to prove that the land required to be dedicated for a park or school site was to meet a need solely attributable to the anticipated influx of people into the community to occupy this particular subdivision (137 N.W.2d 447).

The *Jordan* court required, as a test of reasonableness, that the Village establish a rational nexus between the exactions and the public park needs created by the new subdivision.

The *Jordan* case was followed by a series of New Jersey cases upholding the rational nexus test.[13] Under this rule the subdivider only assumes those costs which bear a rational linkage to the needs created by and the benefits conferred upon the subdivision. While the *Pioneer Trust* test relates solely to a developer's specific proposal, the "rational nexus" test allows for the added apportionment of cost within the near future when a developer's activity continues into that future. This is clearly recognized in *Jordan,* where the court concluded:

> *** a required dedication of land for school, park or recreational sites as a condition for approval of the subdivision plat should be upheld as a valid exercise of police power if the evidence reasonably establishes that the municipality will be required to provide more land for schools, parks and playgrounds as a result of approval of the subdivision (137 N.W.2d 448).

The trend toward ratification of park and fee-in-lieu exactions received additional impetus in *Jenad v. Village of Scarsdale,* 218 N.E.2d 673 (N.Y. 1966). At issue in the case was a resolution of the planning commission which stated:

The Commission may require adequate, convenient and suitable areas for parks or playgrounds, or other recreational purposes, to be set aside in the subdivision and to be dedicated to the Village, as provided for by 179-1 of the Village Law. No arbitrary percentage of area shall be insisted upon by the Commission, but, in general, subdividers will be required to set aside up to 10 percent of the area for these purposes. After considering the character and recreational needs of the neighborhood in which the subdivision is located, the suitability of land in the subdivision for park and playground purposes . . . the Commission may direct and determine that cash is to be deposited in lieu of land dedications for park, playground and recreational purposes. In such event, the Commission shall require a cash deposit of $250 for each lot in the subdivision.[14]

The New York court relied upon *Jordan* and *Billings* to sustain the fee as a reasonable burden on the developer.

§3.5. Reasonably Related Test

The most liberal standard used to measure the legitimacy of subdivision exactions is the "reasonably related" test that arose from case law in California. The California Supreme Court's decision in *Associated Home Builders of the Greater East Bay, Inc. v. City of Walnut Creek*, 484 P.2d 606 (Calif 1971) is regarded as the seminal case for this test. The court ruled that so long as the park land or fees exacted "bear a reasonable relationship to the use of the facilities by the future inhabitants of the subdivision," the mandated dedication is valid. In relying on an earlier decision the court rejected the Association's contention that the dedications could be justified only if the particular need were attributable to the population increase created solely by that subdivision.[15] In rejecting the Pioneer Trust test the court found a reasonable connection between the land needs and projected population increases in the subdivision.

Under this test, the court presumes the ordinance is valid and the burden of demonstrating unreasonableness of the dedication shifts to the subdivider. The subdivider must prove that there is no sensible connection between the subdivision and the exaction.[16] This "reasonably related" test was recently affirmed in *City of College Station v. Turtle Rock Corp.*, 680 S.W.2d 802 (Tx 1984). In reversing a lower court decision the court outlined the standard for review of reasonableness:

. . . the court must consider whether there is a reasonable connection between the increased population arising from the subdivision development and the increased park and recreation needs in this neighborhood. The burden rests on Turtle Rock to demonstrate that there is no such reasonable connection.

Both need and benefit must be considered. Without a determination of need, a city could exact land or money to provide a park that was needed long before the developer subdivided his land. Similarly, unless the court considers the benefit, a city could, with monetary exactions, place a park so far from the particular subdivision that the residents received no benefit. *** The following are examples of the types of evidence which the court may consider: size of lots in the subdivision, the economic impact on the subdivision, the amount of open land consumed by the development (680 S.W.2d 804).

At issue in this case was the city's dedication requirement of one acre of land per 133 dwelling units. In applying the "reasonably related" test to this ordinance the court agreed with the city's position that the ordinance was reasonable on its face. Subsequent to the 1971 California decision in *Walnut Creek,* a number of other courts have considered the constitutional test to be applied in reviewing park land dedication ordinances. The majority of those decisions have applied the "reasonably related" test. The following states have adopted the reasonably related test.

California.	*Associated Home Builders of the Greater East Bay, Inc. v. City of Walnut Creek,* 484 P.2d 606 (1971).
Kansas.	*Coronado Dev. Co. v. City of McPherson,* 368 P.2d 51 (1962).
Minnesota.	*Collis v. City of Bloomington,* 246 N.W.2d 19 (1976).
Missouri.	*Home Builders Assoc. of Greater Kansas City v. City of Kansas City,* 555 S.W.2d 832 (1977).
Texas.	*City of College Station v. Turtle Rock Corp.,* 680 S.W.2d 802 (1984).
Utah.	*Call v. City of West Jordan,* 614 P.2d 1257 (1980).
Wyoming.	*Coulter v. City of Rawlins,* 662 P.2d 888 (1983).

C. SPECIAL PROBLEMS AND SAFEGUARDS

Although a number of cases have dealt with adopting a constitutional test of "reasonableness" of the subdivision exactions, a significant number of other issues have also been examined. Issues relating to the acreage of dedicated lands, the validity of fees in lieu of land, the importance of planning and the relationship of impact fees have been addressed by the courts. Case results vary on these issues but certain patterns exist to serve as guideposts for municipalities dealing with these issues. The following sections deal with these problems.

§3.6. Necessity of Park Plan

In planning, the comprehensive plan is the blueprint for regulations and the regulations should be in conformance with the plan. In the zoning cases, however, the courts have not universally accepted the "plan first" rule or that the "regulations must conform" to the plan rule. What then is the role of the comprehensive park and recreation plan in the subdivision control process? The more recent case law on mandatory dedication is instructive on pointing out the need for an adequate plan.

The necessity of relating subdivision exactions to the needs identified in the park plan is illustrated in *City of Fayetteville v. IBI, Inc,* 659 S.W.2d 505 (Ark 1983). In reviewing the city's cash-in-lieu-of-land requirement, the Arkansas Supreme Court held that the city did not have a sufficiently definite plan regarding park facilities to justify the cash exaction sought from the developer. Some of the findings of the court regarding the plan are noteworthy.

> Under Fayetteville's Comprehensive Land Use and Public Facilities Plan the territory within the planning commission's jurisdictions is divided into four districts, which are each subdivided into several neighborhoods. With respect to public parks, the planning commission projected the maximum possible residential population for each neighborhood by 1990. It then determined the number of acres of public parks that would be needed in each neighborhood if and when the maximum was reached. By subtracting the existing park acreage from the projected need, the planning commission determined the park acreage that would be needed in each neighborhood if it reached its maximum potential. ** So far, the Fayetteville plan is nothing more than a broad statement of possibilities for the future. *** But that is all.
>
> No location for any future park has been determined. Such locations will be decided on a case-by-case basis, as the particular area develops in the future (659 S.W.2d 507).

Based on this uncertainty the court concluded that no plan was in effect in Fayetteville.

The Fayetteville case is a barometer of the increased weight given by courts around the United States to the comprehensive plan. For other cases where the plan was critical see *Associated Home Builders v. City of Walnut Creek,* 484 P.2d 606 (Calif 1971) and *Save El Toro Assoc. v. Davis,* 141 Cal. Rptr. 282 (Calif 1977).

An adequate comprehensive plan may avoid a contention that the park site selection for the dedication was arbitrary or unreasonable.[17] It prevents a salt and pepper approach to needs and provides a developer with some idea of how the subdivision fits into the whole community.[18] A park and recreation plan should contain policies, park land standards and criteria adopted by the community, park land needs and deficiencies by geographical area with some specificity as to park locations, and a schedule for meeting those identified needs. The derivations of the park standards should be clearly evident and there must be a reasonable relationship between the needs created by the population growth and the park land required to meet the burdens created by that growth.

§3.7. Park Acreage Formulas

Although the modern trend is to uphold park land dedication requirements as constitutional, an ordinance may be declared confiscatory if the exactions require an excessive and unreasonable dedication of property or cash. The problem confronting the draftsman of a park dedication ordinance is to develop a formula and land requirement that will pass constitutional muster. Under the "rational nexus" and "reasonably related" tests, once a municipality has established the judicially required relationship between its exaction and the needs and benefits of the proposed subdivision, the burden of providing contravening evidence shifts to the developer. Therefore, it is critical for the municipality to demonstrate that the exaction is related to the additional needs created by the developer's activity and the burden of meeting those needs is reasonably cast upon the developer.

Although in many cases the courts have examined the "reasonableness" of the amount of land dedicated, the case law provides little help in determining the exact amount of land to dedicate. Courts have reviewed ordinance requirements ranging from three percent to 12 percent of the land in the development with mixed results.[19] Whatever formula is used, it is clear that the ordinance should contain standards which apportion the exactions according to the reasonable recreation needs of the neighborhood to be served.

Two principal formulas have been used for determining the basis and amount of land to be dedicated in subdivision ordinances: (1) a fixed percentage based on the amount of land in the subdivision and (2) a population formula where a given amount of land is required for a certain number of people. Under either approach, the draftsman must relate the formula to neighborhood needs and benefits generated by the developer's activity.

Fixed Percentage Formula. Under this formula, a developer is required to dedicate a certain percentage of land based on the overall size of the development. The major advantages of this formula are simplicity and ease in calculation of the land to be dedicated.

Several commentators have criticized this approach, suggesting that it is inherently suspect.[20] They argue that such a formula does not relate needs to benefits and as such is not necessarily a reasonable measure to determine the dedication requirement. A municipality that adopts a fixed percentage requirement without relating the exaction to the increased needs created by that developer may have difficulty meeting the "rational nexus test" or "reasonably related test." For example, a planning commission regulation that developers of residential plats dedicate at least seven percent of the plat area to the city was held to be arbitrary in *Frank Ansuini, Inc. v. Cranston,* 264 A.2d 910 (R.I. 1970). The specific provision of the planning commission's rules and regulations provided:

> Developers of residential plats shall deed at least seven (7) per cent of the land area of such plat to the city to be used for recreation purposes.*** Such land shall be chosen on the basis of a preliminary site plan showing the entire area of land to be subdivided at present or in the future. Such land shall be chosen so as to be adaptable for such purposes, must be in a desirable location and must be acceptable to the Plan Commission (264 A.2d 912).

After finding that the city had the enabling authority to require land dedications the court concluded that the seven percent formula used to calculate the land requirement was arbitrary on its face. The court went on to state that the city could exact only that amount of land resulting from specific and unique activity attributable to the developer and seven percent was not attributable to the developer.

A similar result was reached two years later in *Admiral Development Corp. v. City of Maitland,* 267 So.2d 860 (Fla 1972). The developer challenged the land dedication formula which required that "when lands are subdivided within the city at least five percent (5%) of the gross area of such lands shall be dedicated by the owner to the city." The Florida court recognized the need for park land in new subdivision development and found it commendable that the city sought to act in the furtherance of this need. The court concluded, however, that the ordinance's provisions and the five percent flat rate dedication would permit the exercise of unbridled discretion by the city. Citing with approval the *Ansuini v. Cranston* rationale the court found that a flat rate formula could not be reconciled with the need for the land requirement.

The validity of the fixed percentage formula as a means of relating needs and benefits was recently addressed in *J.E.D. Assoc. v. Town of Atkinson,* 432 A.2d 12 (N.H. 1981). In this case, a seven and one-half percent formula was held to be unreasonable in that it did not reasonably relate the size of the development to the needs generated by the developer's activity.

Not all courts have rejected the fixed percentage formula, but they have carefully reviewed the relationship between need created and benefit provided in the context of the formula. The more contemporary fixed percentage formulas have avoided the rigidity presented in the Ansuini and Admiral cases by giving developers the opportunity to pay a cash equivalent. Thus, in *Call v. City of West Jordan,* 614 P.2d 1257 (Utah 1980) the court upheld a city ordinance which required developers to dedicate seven percent of the proposed subdivision land for parks or alternatively to pay the city a cash equivalent. In its reasoning the court found that the seven percent requirement could not be applied without the developers being given the opportunity to present evidence to show that seven percent had unreasonable relationships to the needs for parks created by their subdivision. On this basis the court was willing to uphold the ordinance.

In 1976 the Minnesota Supreme Court in *Collis v. City of Bloomington,* 246 N.W.2d 19 (Minn 1976) upheld a city ordinance requiring a dedication of 10 percent of subdivision property for parks. The ordinance used the 10 percent formula as a guide and attempted to relate park needs to benefits. Pertinent parts of the ordinance provided:

> *Park Donation.* It is hereby found and declared that, as a general rule, it is reasonable to require an amount of land equal in value to (10) percent of the undeveloped land proposed to be subdivided, be dedicated or reserved to the public for public use for parks and playgrounds. As an alternative, the subdivider may contribute an amount in cash equivalent to the value of land required to be dedicated by this subdivision, except that where the total land involved is less than 30 acres the City shall have the option as to whether cash or land be donated to meet this requirement (246 N.W.2d 21).

Apparently the record demonstrated that the city had made a showing that 10 percent was not unreasonable in relation to the property of the developer. The court stated that a 10 percent requirement might be arbitrary as a matter of law if it does not reasonably relate needs and benefits created by a particular subdivision, but concluded that such a holding would be premature. On its face, the ordinance says only that "as a general rule, it is reasonable to require" dedication of 10 percent of the land or payment of 10 percent of undeveloped land value." Certainly a developer may rebut this statement in a judicial review proceeding under Minn. St. §462.361 in which all of the facts and the developer's constitutional claims may be fully developed. So construed, the statement in the ordinance regarding a 10 percent dedication or donation does not render the ordinance unconstitutional.

These jurisdictions have upheld the fixed percentage formula.

Connecticut.	*Aunt Hack Ridge Estates Inc. v. City of Danbury,* 273 A.2d 180 (1970).
Massachusetts.	*Creative Environments Inc. v. Estabrook,* 491 F.Supp. 547 (1980).
Missouri.	*Home Builders Association of Greater Kansas City v. City of Kansas City,* 555 S.W.2d 832 (1977).
Montana.	*Billings Properties Inc. v. Yellowstone County,* 394 P.2d 182 (1964).
New York.	*East Neck Estates Ltd. v. Luchsinger,* 305 NY.S.2d 922 (1969).

Population Based Formula. Any formula that relates the exactions imposed on the developer to needs and benefits based on the number of people in the proposed development is superior to a flat percentage formula.[21] In theory, the most scientific way to relate the quantity of land to be dedicated to the need for the use of such land would be to require a park plan for each subdivision. Such a provision would be expensive, time consuming and subject to abuse by local officials. It would not provide the developer with a definitive standard as to the land subject to dedications nor assure equal treatment for developers.

There are two major types of population-based formulas used to determine park exactions: (1) a required acreage of land based on the number of dwelling units in or density of the subdivision or (2) a required acreage per 1000 population.[22] Under either formula the population in the development, rather than geographical size of the development, determines the size of the exaction.

The more recent appellate court decisions generally have affirmed population-based standards. This formula was at issue in *Home Builders Association of Greater Kansas City v. City of Kansas City,* 555 S.W.2d 832 (Mo 1977) and *City of College Station v. Turtle Rock Corp.,* 680 S.W.2d 802 (Tx 1984). In the Missouri case the Supreme Court held that the ordinance exaction formula of "4 acres per 100 living units" was not unreasonable on its face. The court remanded the case for a new trial and suggested that the attorneys for the subdividers introduce evidence on the fairness of specific exactions as to specific properties. The *Turtle Rock* case involved an ordinance exaction formula of "1 acre of land for each 133 dwelling units." The Texas Supreme Court held that College Station's park land exaction was not "unconstitutionally arbitrary or unreasonable on its face" and remanded the case back to the trial court. At trial, the burden will be on Turtle Rock to prove that the exaction is arbitrary or unreasonable as applied to its development.

The reasonableness of an exaction formula based on acres per 1000 people was an issue in two Florida cases and a Wyoming case. In the 1983 case of *Hollywood, Inc. v. Broward County,* 431 So.2d 606 (Fla 1983) a Florida appellate court upheld a county ordinance that *inter alia* required an exaction of "3 acres of park land for every 1000 residents of the proposed subdivision." The court held that the subdivision exactions for county parks are permissible so long as the exactions are shown to offset, but not exceed, reasonable needs attributable to the new subdivision residents.

In the same year another Florida appellate court followed the same logic in upholding a city exaction of "5 acres per 1000 residents." The court in *Town of Longboat Key v. Lands End, Ltd.,* 433 So.2d 574 (Fla 1983) reversed a decision of the trial court, even after the city had doubled its exaction requirement. At the time the lawsuit was instituted the city had an exaction formula of "2 1/2 acres per 1000 residents." After the lawsuit was filed, but before trial, the city amended its ordinance to remedy a defect and in enacting the amendment increased the exaction formula from two and one-half to five acres per 1000 residents. Nevertheless, the court was unwilling, as a matter of law, to declare this standard to be unreasonable.

Also in 1983, the Supreme Court of Wyoming in *Coulter v. City of Rawlins,* 662 P.2d 888 (Wyo 1983) upheld a population per 1000 formula. The city enacted a comprehensive park dedication ordinance that, among other requirements, imposed an exaction formula of "6 acres per 1000 persons in the subdivision." From a review of numerous park land dedication cases the court found that the city ordinance was reasonably related to lessening the impact on park facilities that result from the influx of inhabitants caused by the development.

§3.8. Fees in Lieu

In the case of small subdivisions, where the land exaction formula does not allow the dedication of a usable tract of land, the fee-in-lieu option offers greater flexibility for the city and the developer. This option may provide the same benefits even for larger developments. Some commentators have concluded that, because it is difficult to establish land dedication criteria that will assure equal treatment for all sizes, types and densities of subdivision and that will fairly apportion the burden between new and existing subdivision residents, the fee exaction is the more equitable, flexible and practical device.[23] Because cash is not as unique as land, fees represent an equitable contribution between the developer with a 50-lot subdivision of single family homes and the developer of an apartment complex with 200 units on the same size area of land. A fee schedule offers further flexibility over a land formula in that the cash can be applied for improvements required to make a park usable, as well as for acquiring additional land.

The fee-in-lieu system has not been immune from a number of legal challenges. Some of the legal pitfalls with the fee-in-lieu system have dealt with the legal authorization of the fees and with time and geographical constraints on the expenditure of the fees. An early line of cases, in which authority to require in-lieu fees was an issue, held that the fees were a tax not specifically authorized by statute. These cases were resolved by application of the "regulatory versus revenue" test. If the fees are classified as a revenue measure, the courts generally find that the fees are without legislative authorization. Illustrative of this analysis is *Haugen v. Gleason,* 359 P.2d 108 (Or 1961) where the Oregon Supreme Court found that a fee of $37.50 per subdivision lot was a revenue measure designed to produce money for public purposes and therefore void as a tax not within the power of the county to levy. The Oregon court reasoned that if the fee was charged merely as a tool in the subdivision regulation process it could be sustained. In reviewing the county ordinance, however, the court concluded that the $37.50 per lot was a revenue source for new parks and was not specifically authorized by the statute. Similar reasoning was used in *Regg Homes Inc. v. Dickerson*, 179 N.Y.S.2d 771 (N.Y. 1958), *Rosen v. Village of Downers Grove*, 167 N.E.2d 230 (Ill 1960), *Coronado Development Co. v. City of McPherson* 368 P.2d 51 (Kan 1962), *West Park Ave. v. Township of Ocean*, 224 A.2d 1 (N.J. 1966), *McKain v. Toledo City Plan. Comm* 270 N.E.2d 370 (Ohio 1971), *Sanchez v. City of Santa Fe*, 481 P.2d 401 (N.M. 1971) and *Hillis Homes Inc. v. Snohomish County*, 650 P.2d 193 (Wash 1982).

A more contemporary and better reasoned line of cases recognizes that provisions for fees in lieu of dedicated land are not taxes and are therefore valid as a regulatory scheme. The genesis for this approach is *Jordan v. Village of Menomonee Falls*, 137 N.W.2d 442 (Wisc 1966). The Wisconsin Supreme Court found that the $200 per lot equalization fee was an exercise of the police power and not in the nature of a tax. In reaching that decision the court held that the fee was an integral component of the regulatory process and not intended as a general revenue measure. The following jurisdictions have followed the Jordan reasoning: *Jenad, Inc. v. Village of Scarsdale*, 218 N.E.2d 673 (N.Y. 1966); *Associated Home Builders of Greater East Bay Inc. v. City of Walnut Creek*, 484 P.2d 606 (Calif 1971); *Board of Education of Dupage County v. Surety Developers, Inc*, 347 N.E.2d 149 (Ill 1975); *Banberry Dev. Corp. v. South Jordan City*, 631 P.2d 899 (Utah 1981); and *Hollywood Inc, v. Broward County*, 431 So.2d 606 (Fla 1983).

Two important questions in determining if the fee-in-lieu provision is a regulation or a tax are "where" and "when" the fees are to be spent. Any ordinance that does not earmark fees to neighborhood park acquisition or development within a reasonable time period is suspect. In *Town of Longboat Key v. Lands End, Ltd.*, 433 So.2d 574 (Fla 1983), the court concluded that if fees collected under the ordinance are not restricted solely for the purpose of acquiring open space and park land in order to meet the needs created by the new development than the fees are an invalid tax.

The necessity of earmarking the fees for the acquisition and development of parks benefiting the new development was considered in *City of College Station v. Turtle Rock Corp.*, 680 S.W.2d 802 (Tx 1984). The city ordinance provided that in those circumstances where an area of less than one acre was required to be dedicated the developer could make a cash payment of $225 per dwelling unit. As a further condition the ordinance required the city to establish a special fund for the cash paid in lieu of dedication and that this cash had to be expended within two years for the acquisition of a neighborhood park. In upholding the ordinance the Texas court acknowledged the legitimate goal of providing neighborhood parks for the development and that reasonable restrictions were placed on the use of the money.

Not only is it important to attach a reasonable time period for the expenditure of the fee but it is also prudent to earmark the money for the benefit of the proposed development. An ordinance that allows the cash to be spent anywhere in the city for any type of park is inherently suspect.[24] The Missouri Supreme Court upheld the geographical earmarking of fees when it approved a Kansas City ordinance requirement that "fees shall be used for the acquisition and development of a park within one half-mile (1/2) of the periphery of the subdivision."[25] While this represents a rigid standard, it does address the problem of geographical earmarking.

Closely related to the issue of earmarking fees is the question of the "reasonableness of the fee" as determined by a particular formula. Obviously, a fee that requires a developer to pay for a substantially larger portion of a park development than is reasonably related to the activity of the new subdivision will not be upheld by the courts. Before turning to the issue of "what is a fair share," it may be helpful to describe the formulas commonly used to determine the fee. There are three major types of formula for calculating a dollar amount for fee-in-lieu provisions: those in which the fees are based upon (1) the fair market value of land in the area; (2) a fixed dollar amount per lot or dwelling unit, and (3) a variable amount based on the density of the subdivision.[26] Whichever formula is used, the fees exacted must comply with the constitutional standard of "reasonableness." Some commentators have discussed this standard based on horizontal equity—similar treatment for those similarly situated.[27] Recently, the Utah Supreme Court attempted in *Banberry Development Corp. v. South Jordan City,* 631 P.2d 899 (Utah 1981) to define the attributes of "reasonableness" by providing seven factors to guide municipalities in setting fees. Those seven factors are:

1. the cost of existing capital facilities;
2. the manner of financing existing capital facilities;
3. the relative extent to which the newly developed properties and the other properties in the municipality have already contributed to the cost of existing capital facilities;
4. the relative extent to which the newly developed properties and the other properties in the municipality will contribute to the cost of existing capital facilities in the future;
5. the extent to which the newly developed properties are entitled to a credit because the municipality is requiring their developers or owners to provide common facilities that have been provided by the municipality and financed through general taxation in other parts of the municipality;
6. extraordinary costs, if any, in servicing the newly developed properties; and
7. the time-price differential inherent in fair comparisons of amounts paid at different times. (631 P.2d 904).

Those factors do not exhaust the extent of a city's deliberation in determining a developer's equitable share, but they offer a point of demarcation for further refinement.

D. SUMMARY

Before a municipality may impose compulsory park land dedication requirements on developers, it must possess the requisite authority. This authority is derived from home rule legislation, or from state enabling statutes patterned after the Standard City Planning Act, the Model Municipal Planning Act or the Model Subdivision Regulation Act. Except in a few states, the enabling legislation does not expressly authorize park land exactions on the developer. In the absence of express authority, courts have implied the authorization from a liberal interpretation of different enabling laws. The clear judicial trend is to imply the authority to impose park exactions.

In exercising the legal authority to impose park land exactions, municipalities must not violate the constitutional requirements of "due process" and "reasonableness." In the context of park land exactions the courts have developed three tests to measure the reasonableness of the exaction: (1) the Specifically and Uniquely Attributable Test, (2) the Rational Nexus Test, and (3) the Reasonably Related Test. The latter two tests provide greater latitude to municipalities and carry with them a presumption of validity, whereas the first test is highly restrictive and shifts the burden of proof on ordinance validity to the municipality. Recent contemporary court decisions have favored the adoption of the rational nexus or reasonably related test.

Developers may be required to meet the cost of a neighborhood's increased park and recreation needs to the extent that the increased need results from the subdivision. A comprehensive park and recreation plan is the document that establishes a community's overall neighborhood park needs and therefore furnishes the justification for the park land exaction. An ordinance that does not rely on the plan to relate the developer's activity to the neighborhood's overall park needs is suspect.

Two formulas have been used to determine the park acreage exaction. The population-based formula should not significantly exceed recognized neighborhood park acreage standards. Formulas in the four to seven acre per 1000 population range have generally been upheld by the courts. Those beyond the seven acres per 1000 are suspect because they are not based on existing planning criteria. Although fixed percentage formulas of up to ten (10) percent of the total development have been upheld, legal commentators have criticized the formula for not taking into account population increases and park needs.

The fee-in-lieu of land provisions offer municipalities and developers an alternative when a land dedication does not provide a usable tract of land.

The in-lieu provision must meet the same standards of reasonableness required of the land dedication. A municipality with unbridled discretion in determining "where and when" the fees collected are to be expended has an inherently suspect regulatory scheme that the courts have not hesitated to find invalid. Reasonable time and geographical conditions must be placed on the expenditure of these fees.

CHAPTER THREE NOTES

1. See generally, Validity and Construction of Regulations as to Subdivision Maps or Plats, 11 A.L.R.2d 524 and Johnson, *Constitutionality of Subdivision Control Exactions: The Quest for a Rationale,* 52 Cornell LQ 871 (1967).
2. E.C. Yokley, *Law of Subdivision,* 2nd ed., (Charlottesville: The Michie Co., 1981), p. 2.
3. 7 Rohan, *Zoning and Land Use Controls,* § 45.01(3), (1984).
4. 56 Am. Jur.2d, Municipal Corps, §127.
5. Charter of Cincinnati, Ohio, Art VII, 8 (1963).
6. Ellickson, *Suburban Growth Controls: An Economic and Legal Analysis,* 86 Yale LJ 385, 473 (1977).
7. See Annot, Validity and Construction of Statute or Ordinance Requiring Land Developer to Dedication Portion of Land for Recreational Purpose, or Make Payment in Lieu Thereof, 43 A.L.R.3d 862 (1972).
8. Comment, *Subdivision Land Dedications: Objectives and Objections,* 27 Stan. LR 419, 432 (1975).
9. Dolbeare, *Mandatory Dedication of Public Sites as a Condition in the Subdivision Process in Virginia,* 9 U. Rich. LR 435, 437 (1975).
10. *Jordan v. Menomonee Falls,* 385 U.S. 4 (1966) and *Assoc. Home Builders v. Walnut Creek,* 404 U.S. 878 (1972).
11. E.g. Johnson, Supra, p. 911.
12. Dolbeare, Supra, p. 439.
13. *Longridge Builders, Inc. v. Planning Board,* 245 A.2d 336 (1968), *Brazer v. Borough of Mountainside,* 262 A.2d 857 (1970).
14. Regulations of the Planning Commission of the Village of Scarsdale, Art 15 Section 6.
15. *Ayers v. City Council of Los Angeles,* 207 P.2d 1 (Calif 1949).
16. *Wald Corp. v. Dade County,* 338 So.2d 863 (Fla 1976).
17. Ferguson and Rosnic, *Judicial Limitations on Mandatory Subdivision Dedications,* 13 Real Est. LJ 250, 261 (1984).
18. Dolbeare, Supra, p. 459.
19. Karp, *Subdivision Exactions for Park and Open Space Needs,* 16 Amer. Business LJ 277, 292 (1979).
20. See generally, Landau, *Urban Concentrations and Land Exactions for Recreational Use: Some Constitutional Problems in Mandatory Dedication Ordinances in Iowa,* 22 Drake LR 71, 95 (1972), Johnson, *Constitutionality of Subdivision Control Exactions: The Quest for Rationale,* 52 Cornell LQ 871, 924 (1967), Heyman and Gilhool, *Constitutionality of Imposing Increased Community Costs*

on New Suburban Residents through Subdivision Exactions, 73 Yale LJ 1119, 1142 (1964).

21. Heyman and Gilhool, Supra, pp. 1142-1143.
22. See M. Brooks, "Mandatory Dedication of Land or Fees-in-Lieu of Land for Parks and Schools," American Society of Planning Officials Report No. 266, Feb 1971, pp. 10-13.
23. Heyman and Gilhool, Supra, p. 1142.
24. *Town of Longboat Key v. Lands End, Ltd.*, 433 So.2d 574 (Fla 1985), *Collis v. City of Bloomington*, 246 N.W.2d 19 (Minn 1976), *Gulest Assoc. v. Town of Newberry*, 15 A.2d 815 (N.Y. 1960).
25. *Home Builders Association of Greater City v. City of Kansas City*, 555 S.W.2d 832 (Mo 1977).
26. Brooks, Supra, pp. 13-15.
27. Ellickson, *Suburban Growth Controls: An Economic and Legal Analysis*, 86 Yale L.J. 385 (1977) and Rundus, *The Permissible Scope of Compulsory Requirements for Land Development in Colorado*, 54 Univ. of Colorado LR, 447 (1983).

CHAPTER FOUR
The Park and Recreation Plan

A. PLAN PREPARATION

§4.1. The Comprehensive Plan

A park and recreation plan is a component of a community's overall comprehensive plan. The comprehensive general plan is the generic document upon which public and private decisions affecting the physical form and future quality of life within a community are made. From a planner's perspective, there are many definitions as to what constitutes a comprehensive plan. Goodman and Fruend define it as "an official public document adopted by a local government as a policy guide to decisions about the physical development of a community."[1] The plan indicates in a general way how the community will develop in the next 20 to 30 years. It serves as a guide for all regulatory and infrastructure decisions which will affect the growth pattern of the community.[2] Beal and Hollander identified five specific characteristics of the comprehensive plan: (1) it is a physical plan; (2) it is long range; (3) it is truly comprehensive; (4) it is a statement of policy; (5) it is a guide to decision-making.[3] In a more general sense Gold defines the comprehensive plan as "a general guide to the future character and development of a community." It identifies significant areas to be preserved or changed to achieve social, economic, or environmental goals.[4]

A comprehensive plan is a policy document rather than a precise physical plan depicting exactly how the future land use pattern will emerge. The plan may contain a future land use map and may specify such elements as thoroughfares, flood plains, and specific development constraints such as topography, or unique ecological areas to be preserved as community open spaces. However. any specific design and development standards are found as policy statements in the appropriate sections of the plan. The policy role of the plan is to coordinate geographical and functional elements of the community in a unified and consistent manner.

The comprehensive plan serves as a guide for implementing regulations, programs and services and as a management tool with respect to the allocation of community resources. For example, the elected body is guided by the growth management policies in the comprehensive plan when deciding questions of annexation, extension of infrastructure services and the manner in which the area will ultimately develop. In summary, the comprehensive plan serves three basic functions.

1. It is an expression of what the community wants. It is a statement of goals, a listing of objectives and a vision of what might be.
2. It serves as a means for guiding and influencing the many public and private decisions that together form and shape the future community.
3. It may represent the fulfillment of a legal requirement such as the statutory requirement to prepare a comprehensive plan and implement all regulations and programs in accordance with it.[5]

As a policy document, the comprehensive plan is not a design or blueprint. It is organized into a hierarchy of elements, each having a simple, straightforward set of policy statements defining the way in which some event should occur. These policy statements become the guidelines that the Planning Commission, Zoning Commission, Park and Recreation Board, Zoning Board of Adjustment and City Council should use constantly and consistently when reviewing development proposals, zoning requests and site plans. The policies should contain sufficient flexibility to be responsive to changing market conditions without rendering the plan obsolete. For example, policies governing the development of land within and adjacent to flood plains should not change drastically due to trends or fluctuations in the housing market.

Today the more progressive communities are using the comprehensive general plan as the foundation for a combined planning and management system. John Williams, Director of Parks and Recreation for the City of Sunnyvale, California, explains this system and its relationship to the comprehensive general plan.

In Sunnyvale, the General Plan serves as our vision for both short- and long-term council policy setting, budget planning, service delivery, and evaluation. Every decision made by the council today, every major assignment undertaken by staff, is designed to take the city one step closer to implementing a vision, a goal, a general plan of action.

At first glance, the system appears to be simply a collection of actions which most municipalities go through in taking care of city business. That is certainly one function of the system. As a very systematic integration of city activities, the system provides citizens, council and program managers a step-by-step approach to how the governmental process in Sunnyvale operates and their role in that process. But there is more. The system is a rather unique philosophical approach to innovative government. It is designed to

51

operate like a well-oiled machine, with each part working together in initiating and maintaining the city on a course of action that brings citizens quality service.

The system provides the opportunity for the council, citizens and management to collectively develop and initiate a vision for the city through the establishment of goals and policies (policy-making); the implementation of those policies (service delivery); and the opportunity to participate in self-evaluation as to whether those goals and policies were met in the most effective manner possible (evaluation).

The key to our system is the city's General Plan. We came to the conclusion at an early point that the long-range planning of the city had to be the key focus in making short-term (budget) decisions. We felt that if this was not done, the long-term aspirations for our city, as expressed in the General Plan, had no way of occurring. As important, if the General Plan became the key policy document, then a legislative framework would be set which would assist the decisionmakers to think in terms of the long-term implications of priorities expressed in that plan which are not being met to determine where our attention needs to be focused in the coming year.[6]

§4.2. The Park, Recreation and Open Space Element

The form, context and planning process used to prepare this element or chapter of the plan will be influenced by the nature of the local government planning enabling statute and the procedures adopted by the Director of Planning and/or City Manager. The general practice is to treat parks and recreation, more frequently referred to as leisure services, as a separate document or chapter. Open Space may be incorporated in this element; however, it is generally tied into a more comprehensive conservation or environmental resources element. Ideally all three should be addressed in the same chapter or plan element.

The comprehensive general plan is coordinated under the Director of Planning. Specific elements such as parks, recreation and open space should be prepared by the administrative unit having program and management responsibility for implementation of the major portions of the plan. Overall coordination in a comprehensive planning and management framework is done under the director of planning, working with the park and recreation director, the city manager and the legislative body.

As outlined in Figure 4-1 and reported in the literature, the plan should contain as separate chapters, at least the following: Goals and Objectives, Inventory of Existing Resources and Conditions, Projected Deficiencies, General and Specific Policies, Park and Recreation Standards, Action or Implementation Program, and Monitoring and Revision Program. The planning methodology used to prepare the plan should be outlined in the introduction. It is essential that there be logical consistency throughout the procedure and narrative.

Introduction
Describe objectives and scope of plan
Define legal authority for federal/state programs
Define agency responsible for preparation of plan
Describe previous and future studies related to plan
State assumptions and qualifications of plan

Existing conditions
Describe regional context of planning area
Describe leisure behavior patterns of population
Describe environmental characteristics of planning area
Describe recreation problems and potentials/planning unit
Describe general character of planning units

Recreation resources
Classify resources and opportunities
Inventory existing land, facilities, and program
Evaluate opportunities by planning unit
Describe potential recreation resources/programs
Evaluate design, access, and public safety

Demand and use patterns
Inventory time budgets of population
Analyze recreation use patterns by demographic groups
Describe user preference/satisfaction
Analyze causes for nonuse of existing opportunities
Describe problems of special populations
Assess impact of nonresidents/tourists
Assess impact of fees and charges on demand patterns
Assess impact of access on use of facilities

Needs analysis
Analyze demand/supply relationships
Develop use concepts, principles, and design criteria
Develop space, development, and program standards
Describe deficiencies by planning unit
Project needs by planning period and planning unit
Describe public/private potentials to accommodate needs

Goals, policies, and alternatives
Describe existing goals, objectives, and policies
Describe desirable goals, objectives, and policies
Analyze alternative ways to achieve desirable goals
Describe the implications of each alternative
Recommend one alternative
Describe social and environmental impact of alternative

Implementation
Describe public/private actions by project/planning unit
Schedule actions by time period, planning unit, responsibility
Estimate benefits and costs of each project or program
Relate costs to general and capital improvements budgets
Describe needed financing
Describe needed new legislation or responsibility
Describe public participation to approve and implement plan
Describe how, when, and who will revise plan

Figure 4-1 Park and recreation plan elements (Adapted from F So and others, eds., *The Practice of Local Government Planning,* Washington, D.C.: International City Management Assoc., 1979, p. 288).

The goals and objectives set the tone for the plan and should reflect the general findings of the needs assessment. Many planners take the position that their planning process is "future issue driven." Issues vary, and generally point to specific objectives or situations to be addressed in the plan. Williams noted several issues for parks and recreation which are addressed in that element of the Sunnyvale, California Comprehensive Plan:

1. Establish realistic standards for open space for the city in the future.
2. Establish a policy for the acquisition of all school space that might be sold.
3. Provide for cooperation with regional and other governmental agencies to assure adequate regional open space in the future.
4. Set forth a basis for cooperation with industry to assess industrial needs as they relate to open school space to assure its greatest use.
5. Provide for improved maintenance of open school space to assure its greatest use.
6. Encourage the private sector to develop open space and recreation facilities for residents.[7]

Figure 4-2 illustrates examples of goals and objectives for parks, recreation and open space developed by the City of Austin, Texas, as part of their comprehensive planning process. These were developed in response to citizen input which helped identify a range of issues to be addressed in the plan. Figure 4-3 illustrates specific goals and objectives developed in the master plan for parks and recreation.

The park standards section of the plan is essential if the municipality uses the park land dedication authority in subdivision regulations. In this context a standard is defined as a minimum acceptable unit of space for a particular use or activity. Thus, the allocation of space for a variety of land uses within a community is determined by some form of space standard. Space standards relate people (residents of the community) to land (space) for recreation and leisure activities. Facility standards are used to determine the amount of space needed for a recreation facility and its associated activities, for example ball diamonds or tennis courts. The National Recreation and Park Association (NRPA) currently provides guidelines for adopting a space standard, but in recognition of the uniqueness of each community, it leaves to the community the choice of that standard which best fits the local need for parks, recreation and open space. The NRPA also defines various sizes and types of parks, i.e. neighborhood park/playground, including suggested use, service area, desirable size, acres/1000 population and desirable site characteristics. These can be used as recommended or modified to accommodate unique community situations. (See Appendix E for a further discussion of standards).

GOAL 610.0   PROVIDE ADEQUATE PARK LAND AND OPEN SPACE TO MEET THE NEEDS OF AUSTIN'S CITIZENS.

    Objective 611.0   Prepare a parks and recreation master plan for the city.

    Objective 612.0   Expand programs to secure adequate park land and open space to meet a plan adopted by the City of Austin.

    Objective 613.0   Identify and preserve areas of unique natural beauty, significant habitats of flora and fauna, and areas of historical, geological and archaeological significance..

GOAL 620.0   IMPROVE DESIGN CRITERIA AND EVALUATION PROCEDURES TO ACCOMPLISH A HIGH QUALITY PARK SYSTEM.

    Objective 621.0   Establish design criteria for park facilities and programming.

    Objective 622.0   Consider the mobility-impaired population of Austin in all planning and construction phases.

    Objective 623.0   Consider the aesthetic setting of Austin in the planning and development of parks, open space and municipal projects.

    Objective 624.0   Utilize citizen participation to evaluate programs and facilities related to parks, open space and leisure activities.

GOAL 630.0   PROVIDE LEISURE FACILITIES AND RECREATIONAL PROGRAMS TO BEST MEET THE NEEDS OF AUSTIN CITIZENS.

    Objective 631.0   Provide athletic facilities to fulfill the leisure needs of Austin citizens.

    Objective 632.0   Provide facilities and programs for senior citizens so that their increased leisure time can be used to maintain mental and physical health.

    Objective 635.0   Maintain and develop facilities to allow interpretations of the culture, heritage and natural phenomena of the community.

GOAL 640.0   IMPROVE MAINTENANCE PROGRAMS FOR PARKS, OPEN SPACE AREAS AND LEISURE FACILITIES.

    Objective 641.0   Continue efficient maintenance of parks and public open space.

    Objective 642.0   Ensure adequate revenue for the operation of parks, open space and leisure facilities.

    Objective 643.0   Provide for the security and safe use of all park facilities by the genera public.

Figure 4-2. General Park Goals and Objectives. (Taken from Austin, Texas, Tomorrow Comprehensive Plan, 1980. pp. 76 & 84).

PARKS, RECREATION
AND OPEN SPACE

Goals and Objectives

CONTRIBUTE TO THE BETTER-
MENT OF THE QUALITY OF LIFE
IN AUSTIN BY COORDINATING
THE DEVELOPMENT OF A COM-
PREHENSIVE, NONDISCRIMINA-
TORY SYSTEM OF RECREATION
AND LEISURE SERVICES INVOLV-
ING BOTH CURRENT AND POTEN-
TIAL, PUBLIC AND PRIVATE
SERVICE PROVIDERS AND BY
PLAYING A MAJOR ROLE IN THE
DELIVERY OF RECREATION AND
LEISURE SERVICES TO THE AUS-
TIN COMMUNITY

Provide a diverse program of
structured and non-structured recreation services;

Acquire, manage and promote the
use of a network of parks, open
spaces and greenbelts;

Provide a wide range of high quality, well-maintained, and accessible public recreation facilities;

Insure equal opportunity in recreation participation regardless of
race, income, sex, geographic location or physical ability.

PROTECT AND ENHANCE THE
NEIGHBORHOOD SPIRIT IN AUS-
TIN THROUGH AWARENESS OF
UNIQUE GEOGRAPHIC AND CUL-
TURAL SUB-COMMUNITIES

Acquire and develop parks of an
appropriate scale and function at
the neighborhood level;

Establish recreation outreach facilities at the neighborhood level;

Coordinate with the Independent
School Districts to provide focus
and activity centers in rapidly developing neighborhoods;

Coordinate with existing neighborhood organizations on planning
projects that are within their
sphere of influence.

PROVIDE LEADERSHIP FOR THE
COMMUNITY IN THE MAINTE-
NANCE OF A VITAL AND HAR-
MONIOUS ENVIRONMENT BY
SEEKING A LEVEL OF COMPATI-
BILITY BETWEEN MAN-MADE
AND NATURAL SYSTEMS

Identify, acquire and manage in the
public interest unique natural, cultural and historic areas within Austin, particularly along the natural
drainage system;

Encourage and participate in governmental efforts at all levels to
manage growth, plan land use and
regulate environmental pollution;

Manage and maintain existing
parkland in a manner sensitive to
the demands of users and of the
natural environment;

Develop an effective network of
potential guardians of open space
including private interests and
other public agencies;

Participate in the development of
alternative transportation networks
for pedestrians and bicyclists.

PROMOTE NATURAL, FISCAL
AND HUMAN RESOURCE CON-
SERVATION BY COORDINATING
WITH OTHER RECREATION SERV-
ICE PROVIDERS AND PUBLIC EN-
TITIES AND BY ELIMINATING
WASTEFUL, INEFFICIENT USE OF
RESOURCES

Strive to avoid duplication of services and unfair competition with
the private and semi-private sector.

Provide incentives for employees
to be energy efficient.
Evaluate standard departmental
practices for resource waste.

Utilize appropriate technologies on
all new facility designs to render
structures energy and resource efficient.

UPHOLD THE PUBLIC TRUST BY
BEING AWARE OF AND RESPON-
SIVE TO THE RECREATION
NEEDS AND DESIRES OF THE
CITIZENS OF AUSTIN THROUGH
A DEPARTMENTAL PROGRAM OF
CITIZEN PARTICIPATION

Maintain an open dialogue with
concerned neighborhood organizations;

Institute a program of volunteerism
on a neighborhood level;

Utilize citizen input in the planning process;

Continue to work closely with the
Parks and Recreation Advisory
Board.

**Figure 4-3. Specific Park Goals and Objectives in a Park Master Plan. (Taken
from Austin Parks and Recreation Master Plan, 1980, p. 4.).**

With respect to park and recreation standards applied in the context of mandatory park exactions, courts generally accept reasonable space standards and uphold their validity. These standards should be clearly identified in the park and recreation element of the comprehensive plan and the subdivision regulations should be in accordance with the plan. Unless the plan is deficient in a required element, or the enabling statute specifically directs the manner in which that element be prepared, judges prefer not to substitute their judgment for that of the professional planners. To reinforce this judicial deference to planners the following guidelines are suggested.

1. Incorporate the methods and procedures for arriving at the community park land standard in the plan process chapter of the park and recreation and/or open space policy plan element of the comprehensive general plan. If, for example, a standard of six acres of parkland/1000 persons is promulgated, then the procedure used to reach this figure should be shown. Such a standard can be attacked on the grounds that it is arbitrary, capricious or excessive and is not specifically related to a demonstratable need for the park land acres required. A defensible procedure for assessing current trends, needs and deficiencies can be used to overcome this attack.
2. The standard, typology and siting criteria set forth in the plan should be incorporated in the body of the ordinance. This provides a direct link with the comprehensive plan policies, thereby strengthening the validity of the ordinance.
3. The procedures used to monitor the performance of plan policies, standards and criteria should be clearly stated in the explanation of the plan process. This will clearly demonstrate that the standards are current, reasonable and that as applied they provide adequate park land and facilities to meet the recreational needs of the citizenry.
4. The absence of any of the above in the plan and/or ordinance leaves the standard vulnerable to attack.

§4.3. The Planning Process

Park and recreation planning fits the generally accepted planning process models which have emerged from nearly two decades of activity at the federal, state and local level. There is no "perfect" model and it is not our intent to suggest one. Two models are presented for reference and consideration. Figure 4-4 is the planning process model developed and used by the City of Austin, Texas to prepare and update the parks and recreation policy plan. Figure 4-5 is a planning process model which shows a progression of activities which incorporates the policy plan and site or physical plans for individual units within the park, recreation and open space system.

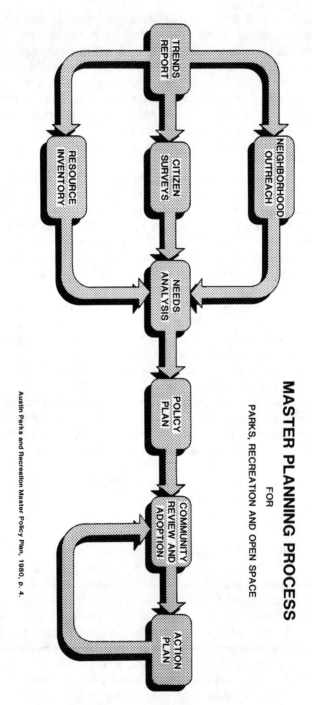

MASTER PLANNING PROCESS

FOR

PARKS, RECREATION AND OPEN SPACE

TRENDS REPORT

RESOURCE INVENTORY

CITIZEN SURVEYS

NEIGHBORHOOD OUTREACH

NEEDS ANALYSIS

POLICY PLAN

COMMUNITY REVIEW AND ADOPTION

ACTION PLAN

Austin Parks and Recreation Master Policy Plan, 1980, p. 4.

Figure 4-4 A park and recreation planning process.

58

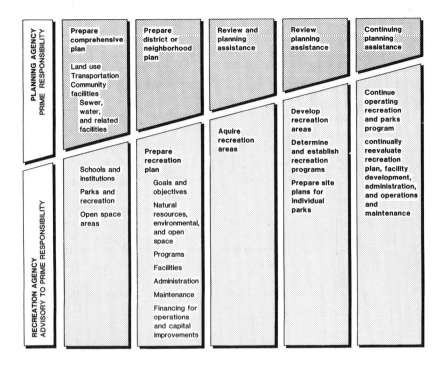

Figure 4-5 A comprehensive planning framework (Adapted from F. So and others, eds., *The Practice of Local Government Planning*, Washington, D.C.: International City Management Assoc., 1979).

B. LEGAL CONSIDERATIONS

§4.4. Statutory Authority for Planning

Cities and counties are empowered to prepare comprehensive general plans as part of their general home rule powers, or through general state enabling legislation. The initial enabling statute was the Standard Planning Enabling Act, prepared as a model statute by the U.S. Department of Commerce in 1926. Many states enacted the model statute specifically for municipalities, and subsequently extended this specific statutory authority to counties.

The planning enabling statute can be broad and general or extremely specific with respect to required and optional plan elements. With general statutes the municipalities and counties may select from a variety of process models and content frameworks. Specific statutes such as found Florida provide specific direction for plan content.

The Florida code provides a definition of the comprehensive plan, defines how the plan is to be adopted and sets forth the legal effect of the plan. The code also provides for required and optional elements of the comprehensive plan, including required studies and surveys. Parks and recreation are addressed in a required element. The statute requires the local general plan to have:

> A recreation and open space element indicating a comprehensive system of public and private sites for recreation, including but not limited to, natural reservations, parks and playgrounds, parkways, beaches and public access to beaches, open spaces, and other recreational facilities.[8]

Passive open space and landscape preservation is addressed in a conservation element.

> A conservation element for the conservation, development, utilization and protection of natural resources in the area, including, as the situation may be, air, water, estuarine marshes, soils, beaches, shores, flood plains, rivers, lakes, harbors, forests, fisheries and wildlife, minerals, and other natural and environmental resources.[9]

The Florida code is representative of the more contemporary local government planning enabling statutes. Key features include provisions for formal adoption, internal consistency, interdepartmental and intergovernmental coordination, and the specific requirement that regulatory, taxing, spending and eminent domain powers be applied in accordance with the plan policies.

§4.5. Legal Status of the Plan

Along with the trend to update the state planning enabling statutes there has been a growing recognition by the judiciary that the plan is a legal document. The courts have been asked to examine, among other things, local government compliance with procedural and substantive requirements of the enabling statute as well as the internal consistency requirement as it pertains to specific regulatory and related actions. Much of the current litigation focuses on the state requirement that zoning and subdivision regulation be consistent with the local policy plans.

The shift from the master plan to the comprehensive general policy plan has occurred in conjunction with a gradual evolution in zoning resulting in flexible zoning, performance zoning, development codes and the growing use of negotiated settlements, which are often in a form of specific use or floating zone. Thus, each zoning case can be decided on the basis of plan policies rather than rigid land use maps.

Judicial interest in the comprehensive plan is best illustrated in the following cases. The Oregon Supreme Court viewed zoning actions as quasi-judicial rather than legislative and placed substantial weight on the comprehensive plan as the basis for zoning changes. In *Fansano v. Board of County Commissioners* 507 P.2d 23, 27 (Ore 1973), the court stated that "the more drastic the change, the greater will be the burden of showing that it is in conformance with the comprehensive plan as implemented by the ordinance." In another major Oregon case involving the relationship of the comprehensive plan to local government zoning the court stated:

> We conclude that a comprehensive plan is the controlling land use planning instrument for a city. Upon passage of a comprehensive plan, a city assumes a responsibility to effectuate that plan and conform prior conflicting zoning ordinances to it. We further hold that the zoning decisions of a city must be in accord with that plan *(Baker v. City of Milwaukee* 553 P.2d 772. (1975)).

The internal consistency issue, involving the manner in which open space policies were considered in county regulations and management surfaced in a 1975 California case, *Coalition for Los Angeles County Planning in the Public Interest v. Board of Superiors of Los Angeles County,* L.A. Co. Super. Ct. No. 63218, 8ERC 1249, (1975). In this case, plaintiffs requested the court to require Los Angeles County to follow state law when preparing and amending the open space policies of the general plan and to implement these policies as they pertained to land use management in a consistent manner. The charges came as a result of the County Planning Commission and County Board of Supervisors failure to act in a manner consistent with the plan policies or to properly amend the plan and policies. The court found procedural and substantive errors and ordered these corrected. In so doing the court reaffirmed the position that the plan and supporting documents be prepared and utilized as directed by the enabling statute. The order further affirmed the principle that citizens should be able to rely on consistent adherence to those plan policies adopted as part of the statutory procedure for preparing and adopting the comprehensive general plan.

C. SUMMARY

The park and recreation element of the comprehensive general plan is the generic planning document upon which the use of the parkland dedication provision of subdivision regulations is predicated. If the power to enact this provision is specifically authorized, does not violate any constitutional protections, and follows the rules fashioned by the state courts, then a properly drafted ordinance carries the presumption of validity. Mandatory park land dedication should be applied in accordance with a comprehensive plan that meets statutory requirements and that would be judged to meet or exceed contemporary planning procedures. References to these have been provided. Park and recreation planners should use them as a guideline, not as a rigid rule. Innovation and flexibility are encouraged, but with the warning that if your plan is challenged, your defense will in part rely on proving you used valued state-of-the-art methods and procedures which are supported by professional organizations and peer professionals.

CHAPTER FOUR NOTES

1. W.I. Goodman, and E.C. Freund, *Principles and Practice of Urban Planning,* (Wash D.C.: International City Management Assoc., 1968). p. 349.
2. Ibid p. 349.
3. F. Beal and E. Hollander, "City Development Plans," in So, Stollman, Beal, and Arnold (eds.), *The Practice of Local Government Planning* (Washington D.C.: International City Management Assoc., 1979), pp. 153-154.
4. S. Gold, *Recreation Planning and Design* (NY: McGraw-Hill Book Co., 1980), p. 72.
5. Beal and Hollander, Supra, p. 164.
6. J. Williams, "The Changing Role of Municipal or Local Government as It Relates to Park, Recreation and Leisure Services" in Health, E. (ed.) *Values and Leisure and Trends in Leisure Services,* The Academy of Leisure Sciences (State College, PA: Venture Publishing, Inc., 1983), pp. 98-101.
7. Williams, Supra, p. 91.
8. Fla. Stat. Ann. Vol 8, Title 11, §163.317(7).
9. Ibid.

CHAPTER FIVE
Ordinance Criteria and Considerations

This chapter deals with basic ordinance considerations in formulating a mandatory dedication of park land provision as part of the subdivision plat approval development process. Generally this process applies to those lands within the municipality. However, if state law permits, the jurisdiction may extend its subdivision regulations to lands not yet annexed but within the extraterritorial jurisdiction. This insures that the jurisdiction's standards for park land and recreation facility development will be applied, along with the other development codes, to any subdivision before the land is annexed. This prevents the development of substandard subdivisions on land that will eventually be annexed. Also, it prevents the loss of prime park land or a situation where the jurisdiction must eventually purchase the needed land at an exorbitant price.

A. THE PLAT APPROVAL PROCESS

In basic land use regulation procedure the zoning ordinance regulates land use by establishing zones or districts with uniform or specific requirements, i.e., lot size, set back, height, bulk, density, permitted uses, conditional uses, parking, and landscaping for each development lot within the district. The subdivision platting ordinance governs the land development process. It includes the legal requirements for platting the lots and for preparing, filing and registering the plat. Included in this authority is the power to impose those standards and conditions specifically authorized by the legislature. These requirements and standards are based on two considerations: (1) the health, safety and general welfare of the future residents of the subdivision, with respect to streets, water, sewer, storm drainage, fire hydrants, parks, playgrounds and schools; and (2) reducing the financial burden on hard-pressed communities by requiring the developer to make the initial installation of capital improvements, to be paid for in part by the home purchasers. Upon completion of the subdivision the municipality assumes responsibility for the maintenance and repair of all public facilities.[1] As previously outlined, the platting and subdivision development process may contain provisions for required park land dedication as a condition to final approval of the plat. All requirements, engineering standards and land dedication provisions which are conditional to plat approval, as well as plat review procedures, are contained in the platting ordinances.

The plan is an important linkage which must be clearly evident throughout the process used to review and approve the park land dedication requirements as a condition to final plat approval. In this manner, application of the provisions of the ordinance to a specific plat can be shown to meet the "rational nexus" and "reasonably related" tests.

The distinction between park and open space should be made when calculating the amount of park land to be dedicated from the subdivision plat. Open space, in the form of environmentally sensitive land, historic sites and other special lands, may be reserved or afforded certain protection through zoning, special development permits and subdivision regulations. Development codes and innovative forms of performance zoning offer numerous alternatives for providing not only the required minimum park and recreation space but also considerable open space for amenity purposes and for protecting critical ecological systems and natural landscape features.

B. ORDINANCE PROVISIONS

Implementation of a mandatory dedication requirement within the framework of state law requires careful organization and drafting of the subdivision regulation ordinance. Each jurisdiction is different and, therefore, the requirements will vary according to state statutes, judicial interpretation (case law) and the unique needs of the jurisdiction. The needs for park and recreation land and facilities as well as the characteristics of the indigenous landscape will influence the necessity of including specific provisions. Any requirement must be acceptable, implementable, realistic and based upon current data and state-of-the-art methodology in parks and recreation and land use planning.

§5.1. Purpose and Definition

This section of the ordinance outlines the broad purposes of the regulations in the context of promoting the health, safety and welfare of the community. It is a good practice to define all the technical and legal terms used in the ordinance for which there is a common usage. All planning, design and park and recreation terms should be consistent with those used in technical publications of their respective professional organizations.

The purposes section should clearly state that the developer will be required to dedicate, or reserve, undeveloped land for parks, playgrounds and open space and/or pay a fee in lieu of dedicating the land. It is desirable to state that this requirement is to provide park and recreational facilities to serve the immediate needs of the residents of the subdivision from which the land or fees were exacted. The ultimate development of park and recreation facilities should be in accordance with the parks and recreation master plan, or element of the comprehensive general plan.

§5.2. Land or Fees

The ordinance should specify that dedication of the required land and/or payment of the appropriate fees is a condition for final plat approval and registration. Exemplary language is found in the *Walnut Creek, California Municipal Code:*

> As a condition of approval of a final subdivision map or parcel map, (sometimes the term plat is used) the subdivider (developer) shall dedicate land, pay a fee in lieu thereof, or both, at the option of the city, for park or recreational (or open space) purposes at the time and according to the standards and formula contained in this article (Art. 6, Sec. 10, 602.2).

The requirement should direct that the dedication, in fee simple, be perfected and/or the cash paid in advance of presenting the final plat to the planning commission or appropriate legislative body. The land should be identified as a park and should be shown on all official and development maps of the subdivision.

Generally it should be the responsibility of the park and recreation officials to advise the Planning Commission on whether to accept land, fee or both. Sometimes a developer offers land which is not suitable for park development by virtue of location or site features. In other instances, the developer may wish to pay the cash fee, particularly if a park site serving other subdivisions has already been selected by the jurisdiction. Park and recreation officials should reject any offer of land which is not suitable for development as a neighborhood park or playfield.

§5.3. Computing the Land Requirement

Although park space and open space are frequently used synonymously in planning and statutory construction, they are defined and viewed as distinctly separate categories of land. Open space, in the generic sense, is any undeveloped land where water, vegetation and topography predominate in a variety of states where the predominant form of human use is passive recreation. Frequently open space is not public recreation space and is provided through zoning, easements and private estates.

Park and recreation space, as used in the subdivision platting context, while admittedly open land in nature, is land set aside to provide space and facilities for people to engage in both active and passive recreation. The key distinction is the word "facilities," such as the playgrounds, playfields, jogging tracks, picnic tables and shelters and recreation centers usually incorporated in neighborhood parks and playfields and community parks.

This section of the ordinance specifies the amount of park land to be dedicated. Generally, the section states a formula to be used in calculating the acreage of land to be dedicated by the developer. This formula should be written as the minimum acceptable acreage, unless the existing park land within the defined service area of the proposed subdivision exceeds the general standard. In such a situation the municipality should not require dedication in excess of the standard.

Some ordinances may define the amount of land to be dedicated according to specific needs, such as school parks, neighborhood parks, community parks or special use areas. If so, the amount of land dedicated will vary according to the portion of land allocated to each type of park.

Two principal formulas are used in mandatory park land ordinances for determining the amount of land to be dedicated: (1) a fixed percentage formula based on the amount of land in the subdivision and (2) a population-based formula, where the amount of land required is based on the size or density of the population in the subdivision. As outlined in Chapter Three, the municipality must demonstrate through its comprehensive park and recreation plan or other planning documents that its formula provides needed park land to benefit the proposed subdivision.

Fixed Percentage Formula. In adopting this formula a municipality should avoid exceeding a 10 percent requirement. The 10 percent figure appears to be the upper range that the courts, based on planning guidelines, will accept. Arguably, however, if unique circumstances required a larger amount of land, it could be applied if reasonably related to the development. Examples of fixed percent formulas that have passed judicial review are presented below. The test of reasonableness for evaluating the formula may differ in application from state to state. Therefore, there is no guarantee that the same formula will be upheld in other jurisdictions. They do, however, provide working models that can be adapted to particular situations.

Bloomington, Minnesota:

> (i) Residential Subdivisions. It is hereby found and declared that, as a general rule, it is reasonable to require an amount of land, equal in value to

ten percent of the undeveloped land proposed to be subdivided, be dedicated or reserved to the public for public use for parks, playgrounds, public open space, or storm water holding areas or ponds. As an alternative, the subdivider may contribute an amount in cash equivalent to the value of land required to be dedicated by this Subdivision. The City shall have the option as to whether cash or land be donated to meet this requirement. The cash payments shall be used for the acquisition of land for parks, playgrounds, public open space, or storm water holding areas or ponds, or as otherwise provided by statute. To determine the value of the land to be dedicated, the undeveloped land value shall be used (Bloomington City Code Sec. [B][i]).

West Jordan, Utah:

In addition to all the other requirements prescribed under this ordinance, the subdivider shall be required to dedicate the seven per cent (7%) of the land area of the proposed subdivision to the public use for the benefit and use of the citizens of the City of West Jordan . . . or in the alternative at the option of the governing body of the City, the City may accept the equivalent value of land in cash if it deems advisable (Ord. 33, Sec 9-C-8).

Population-Based Formula. This type of formula is superior to a fixed-percentage in relating needs generated by the developer's activity to subdivision benefits. There are two variants of a population-based formula, a required acreage per 1000 population or a required acreage based on the population density of the development.

Broward County, Florida:

In order to provide lands or funds or both to be used by the County Commission to provide additional regional, subregional and urban parks necessary to meet the need for such county level parks created by additional residential development, a developer must, at the discretion of the County Commission, either:
a. Dedicate land of suitable size, dimension, topography and general character to serve as regional, subregional or urban parks or a substantial portion thereof which will meet County level park needs created by the development. The total amount of land to be dedicated either on or off the development site must equal a ratio of three (3) acres of land for every one thousand (1,000) residents of the development (Ord 77-43, Sec 5-198 [h]).

Differences in population density of developments affect park needs. A 50-acre development with a population density of four persons per acre creates park needs that are different from those with 15 persons per acre. A density-based formula can take into account these differences. Generally the acreage is determined by the development density (dwelling units/acre) and population density (persons/dwelling unit), based on the nature of the units and the population projections which are indicative of current and short-range trends in family size for new construction. Population tables should be documented according to accepted industry figures, demographic projections and the most recent federal census.

A general formula, based on X acres/y population, which is commonly used in many ordinances is:

$$A = \frac{X(acres) \ (D.F. \ x \ No. \ D.U.)}{1000}$$

where:

> A = the area in acres to be dedicated or to be appraised for fee payment
> DF = the density factor (obtained from the demographic data)
> X = the acres/1000 persons set as the community standard
> D.U. = the number of dwelling units proposed for the subdivision.[2]

Density-based population formulas have been used in Dade County, Florida, Austin, Texas and Walnut Creek, California. Pertinent ordinance provisions are reproduced here as examples.

Dade County, Florida:

> The amount of land to be provided shall be based upon the projected population for the area in question and the "Open Space Standard" of 2.75 acres per 1,000 persons. The actual amount of land to be dedicated shall be determined by the following formula but in no case will the dedication be less than 5 acres unless determined to be in the best interest of the county by the Director of Parks and Recreation:

Net Amount of Dedicated Park Land	Total Number of Dwelling Units	No. of Persons Per Dwelling Unit	.00275 Net Acres Per Person
	(=)	(x)	(x)

> A. Determination of the Number of Dwelling Units:
>   The basis of determining the total number of dwelling units shall be either:
>   1. The actual number of dwelling units reflected on the Final Plat and/or permitted by a legally recorded land covenant, or
>   2. The maximum number of dwelling units permitted within the proposed subdivision as based upon zoning regulations.
> B. Determination of Persons/Dwelling Unit (Population Density) For the purposes of this Section, population density, that is, the number of persons per dwelling unit, shall be in general accordance with the latest available census data and consistent with the official map of Dade County indicating seven (7) Major Statistical Areas (a copy is attached as Exhibit B) and the population density therein and shall be projected as follows:

Persons-per-dwelling unit factors

Area	Single-Family	Multi-Family
1	2.65	1.74
2	3.25	2.34
3	3.17	2.53
4	3.07	2.44
5	3.06	2.59
6	3.50	2.48
7	3.31	2.60

The statistical area shall be constantly monitored by the Dade County Planning Department which shall submit to the County Commission revised statistical data when appropriate (Recommended Ordinance for Mandatory Dedication of Park Land, Dade County, Florida, December 18, 1979, p. 6).

Walnut Creek, California:

10-1.602.4. Standards and Formula for Dedication of Land. Where a park or recreational facility has been designated in the City of Walnut Creek's Master Park and Recreation Plan, an element of the General Plan of the City, and is to be located in whole or in part within the proposed subdivision to serve the immediate and future needs of the residents of the subdivision, the subdivider shall dedicate land for a local park sufficient in size and topography to serve the residents of the subdivision. The amount of land to be provided shall be determined pursuant to the following standards and formula:

$$\text{Land} = \text{Average Number of Persons/DU} \times \frac{1000 \text{ Population}}{\text{Park Acreage Standard} \atop (5 \text{ Acres})}$$

(DU means residential dwelling Unit.)

The following table based on the above formula is to be followed:

Typical Dwelling Unit Type	Average Persons per Dwelling Unit	Acreage Requirement per dwelling unit
Single family	4.0 and up	.0200 acres
Single family	3.5-less than 4.0	.0185 acres
Single family	3.0-less than 3.5	.0160 acres
Single family or Multi-family	2.5-less than 3.0	.0135 acres
Multi-family	2.0-less than 2.5	.0110 acres
Multi-family	below 2.0	.0100 acres

Unless there is evidence to the contrary, the following criteria will be used to estimate population. Planned unit developments, apartment condominiums or other residential projects with known floor plans, will be assumed to average one person per bedroom. Otherwise, medium density, single-family projects will be assumed to average 3.0 persons per dwelling unit, low density single-family projects will be assumed to average 3.5 persons per dwelling unit, and projects with densities of less than 1.0 dwelling unit per acre will be assumed to average 4.0 persons per dwelling unit (Walnut Creek Municipal Code Sec. 10-1.602.4).

Austin, Texas

A. The subdivider shall dedicate to the City all parkland as a part of final plat approval. The amount of land required shall be calculated at a rate of not less than five acres of parkland per 1,000 ultimate residents. The following formula shall be used to determine the amount of parkland to be dedicated:

$$\frac{5.0 \times (\text{No. Units}) \times (\text{Persons/Unit})}{1000} = \text{Acres to be dedicated}$$

B. The number of persons per unit shall be based on data compiled by the City and shall be reviewed and adjusted as necessary. The following figures represent the average number of persons per unit by current density categories, and shall be used to calculate parkland dedication.

Gross Density Per Residential Land Area	Persons Per Unit
From 0 to 6	2.8
Over 6 to 12	2.2
Over 12	1.7

C. Where a subdivision plat is submitted for a multi-family residential development and information is not provided concerning the number of units, the City shall assume the highest density allowed in the zoning district applied to the property. If a property is not zoned, the City shall assume a density of twenty-four (24) units per acre (Code of Austin, Texas, Chap 13, Article III, Sec. 13-3-116).

§5.4. Selecting the Site

The location of the park site should be determined by the park and recreation staff, the developer and the planning staff. The selection criteria should consider the suitability of the site for park development, the relationship of the site to population concentrations, and the proximity of the site to other park and recreation lands. Natural features of the site are important in terms of development, carrying capacity, and maintenance. Access and safety also must be considered, particularly if users must cross busy thoroughfares or if the park contains potentially dangerous natural features such as creeks, streams, ponds or other water bodies.

The ordinance also should provide for an on-site inspection of the property by staff at the time the Planning Commission is reviewing the initial sketch plan. Experts such as landscape architects, soil scientists, geologists, foresters and civil engineers may be needed to evaluate the property and/or review and check the developer's data and claims. Although most developers are honest in their representations and presentations, self interest is involved and experience suggests that there is no substitute for field investigation, data verification and a third party independent opinion if conflicting claims or interpretations arise.

In addition to providing for an on-site inspection, the ordinance should list the criteria to be used by the municipality in determining site suitability. The following are some general considerations which will help get the kind of land desired and needed.

Access. The dedicated land must be readily accessible to all subdivision residents. For larger pieces of dedicated land, at least one side of the site should abut a public street for a minimum distance of fifty (50) feet. If public easements are the sole access, they should be wide enough to accommodate two-way traffic or maintenance equipment.

Location. The park and open space land should be located, to the extent possible, so that it equally serves all residents of the development.

Shape. The shape should be suitable to accommodate those park and open space activities appropriate to the location and needs of the residents. The exact shape is variable. An example of an unacceptable piece of land is one that is 30 feet wide and 1500 feet long, unless it is to be developed as a bike route or as a connecting trail to other facilities.

Soils. Soils should be suitable for the intended park and open space uses.

Unity. The intended park and open space land should be in adequately sized areas, which can accommodate the anticipated uses, rather than to have numerous useless smaller pieces.

Utilities. The major piece(s) of dedicated land should be accessible to—but not crossed on or above the surface by—a public street(s), parking lot(s), telephone, power, fuel, water, and sewer lines, etc. If any of these facilities are placed underground, no part of them or their supportive equipment should protrude above ground level.[3]

§5.5. The Fee-in-Lieu Formula

In many situations it may be more desirable for a municipality to have cash rather than land from the plat. By using the cash option a municipality can equitably assess each plat according to its contribution to the service area population and can purchase the appropriate amount of land to develop park and recreation facilities. The developer, as well as the municipality, should be afforded the opportunity to elect the cash option if this is in the best interest of both parties.

There is no universal procedure for setting a rate for the cash assessment in lieu of land to be dedicated. The key issue in setting the rate is to apportion the fees equitably between higher and lower density uses and new and older developments. Two approaches to determine how much the developer should pay are used: (1) the assessed or fair market value of the land or a percentage thereof at a specific point in time; or (2) a fixed dollar amount per lot or dwelling unit. Examples of the two approaches are presented below.

Fair Market Value

Largo, Florida:

> Amount of Fee in Lieu of Land Dedication—When a fee is charged in lieu of dedication, in whole or in part, that fee shall be based on the fair market value of the land which would have been dedicated to the City for park and recreation purposes. The developer shall provide an MAI appraisal of fair market value of the land when appealing any recommendation of the staff for decision of the DCO (Comprehensive Development Code Largo, Florida. Subsec. 5301 [E] [1985]).

Walnut Creek, California:

> 10-1.602.7. Amount of Fee in Lieu of Park Land Dedication. When fee is required to be paid in lieu of park land dedication, the amount of the fee shall be based upon the average estimated fair market value of the land being subdivided or the value of the land which would otherwise be required to be dedicated according to Section 10-1.602.4. The fair market value shall be as determined by the Community Development Department at the time of final map or parcel map approval. If the subdivider objects to the fair market value determination, the subdivider may request the City to obtain an appraisal of the property by a qualified real estate appraiser mutually agreed upon by the City and the subdivider, which appraisal will be considered by the City in determining the fair market value. All costs required to obtain such appraisal shall be borne by the subdivider (Walnut Creek Municipal Code Article 6. Sec. 10-1.602.7).

Mount Prospect, Illinois:

> Criteria for Requiring a Contribution in Lieu of Park and School Sites. Where the resulting site in a proposed subdivision or development is too small to be usable for the purpose intended or where it is inappropriate for park and recreational purposes or a school site, the Village may require the applicant to contribute cash in lieu of the land dedication.

> Fair Market Value. The cash contribution in lieu of land shall be based on the "fair market value" of the acres of land as improved, that otherwise

would have been dedicated as park and recreation or school sites. It has been determined that the present "fair market value" of such improved land in and surrounding the Village is eighty thousand dollars ($80,000.00) per acre and such figure shall be used in making any calculation herein unless the applicant files a written objection thereto (Revised Development Code, Village of Mount Prospect, Illinois Sec. 16.407 [c][4]).

Fixed Dollar Value

Menomonee Falls, Wisconsin:

8.03. Proportionate Payment in Lieu of Dedication.
(1) Where such dedication is not feasible or compatible with comprehensive plan, the subdivider shall in lieu thereof pay to the Village a fee equivalent to the value of the required dedication. Such fee shall be distributed as follows:
   A. $120.00 per residential lot created by the subdivision to be held in a non-lapsing fund for the benefit of the school district or districts in which the plat lies, on the basis of proper appointment between districts where the plat is in more than one district, and to be made available to the appropriate district or districts upon their request.
   B. $80.00 per residential lot created by the subdivision to be placed in a non-lapsing fund to be used for park and recreation area development.

Austin, Texas:

Where, with respect to a particular subdivision, the dedication of land required pursuant to this section does not meet the standards referred to in Section 13-30-117, the subdivider shall deposit with the City a cash payment or letter of credit.
   A. Such deposit shall be placed in a Neighborhood Park and Recreation Improvement Fund established by the City and shall be used by the City and shall be used for the acquisition and/or improvement of neighborhood parks which will be available to and benefit the residents of said subdivision and located within the service area defined by the Parks and Recreation Department.
   B. —
   C. At the option of the subdivider, the amount of money to be deposited shall be determined by one of the following two methods:

1. The amount equal to or exceeding the fair market value, as determined by the Real Estate Division of the City, of the amount of land required under the provisions of Section 13-3-116.
2. An amount as set forth in the schedule below for each dwelling unit to be constructed within the subdivided area. From the effective date of this ordinance until January 1, 1986, the amount of money to be deposited shall be as follows and for each fiscal year thereafter shall be adjusted to reflect current land values in the Austin area.

Gross Density Per Res. Area	Western Sector	Central Sector	Eastern Sector
0-6	$ 840	$ 630	$ 420
6-12	660	495	330
over 12	510	382	255

**Sector Boundaries shall be as defined in the Parkland Dedication Guidelines (Chap. 13-3, Code of Austin, Texas Article III, Div. 4 Park Land Sec. 13-3-18[c][2]).

In some instances the proposed subdivision plat may be adjacent to or within the service radius of an existing park which has sufficient space to meet the apportioned space attributable to the proposed plat. The park may be partially developed and in need of additional improvements and facilities to satisfy the additional use by the soon to be new residents in the service area. Under these conditions the municipality should be able to require the cash dedication to be used to improve this or other parks. If the developer agrees to do this, he may be credited up to one hundred (100%) per cent of the cash fee requirement.

§5.6. Fee Expenditures

Municipalities do not have unbridled discretion as to where and when the fees collected can be spent. Reasonable purpose, time and geographical constraints should be placed on fund expenditures. Procedures should be included in the ordinance providing for the refund of any unexpended fees.

Trust fund. Once dedicated (surrendered) the fee should be deposited in a special park and recreation development fund. A separate account should be set up for each plat from which a fee is exacted. The ordinance should stipulate that the fee money can be used to acquire park land for the subdivision, improve the land or to acquire other lands and facilities which directly benefit the existing or future residents of the subdivision. Exemplary language is provided in the Austin, Texas ordinance.

> Such deposit shall be placed in a Neighborhood Park and Recreation Improvement Fund established by the City and shall be used for the acquisition and/or improvement of neighborhood parks which will be available to and benefit the residents of said subdivision and located within the service area defined by the Parks and Recreation Department (Ordinance No. 13-3-118[a][1985]).

Time Period. The cash should be expended within two to five years following dedication. Under normal real estate sales conditions about one-half of the lots are sold and built upon by the third or fourth year after all of the improvements are completed. The park and recreation department should provide guidelines as to when they would purchase land and initiate improvements. Raw land should be acquired immediately upon plat approval. When land to be acquired is on the comprehensive plan map, but not exacted from a plat, the jurisdiction should pursue options on the property or adopt the right-of-first refusal (see Chap. 6) in order to hold down speculation and to acquire the property at raw land value rather than improved value.

At the end of the time period provided unexpended funds should be refunded. This may be done in several ways, such as:

1. refund to each lot owner a prorata portion, computed on a square footage of area basis;
2. refund the fees to the applicant who made the dedication;
3. refund to the then record owners of the subdivision in the same proportion the size of their lot bears to the total of all lots within the subdivision.

This refunding procedure should recognize the distinction between home owners and owners of undeveloped lots remaining in the subdivision. The latter may be the original developer, builders or individuals with no prior association with the plat at the time of dedication. Problems may also arise if undeveloped lots are replatted or changed to higher density residential uses. In the latter situation the unused fee may be reallocated and the new plat may require payment of additional fees in the form of a development impact fee, based on the higher development density.

Geographical Conditions. As described in Chapter 3, a municipality must legally earmark the expenditure of funds to acquire land or develop facilities to benefit the residents of the subdivision. This geographical earmarking may be based on a park service area, a fixed distance from the development, or may be open ended. The ordinance provisions from College Station, Kansas City and Mt. Prospect are illustrative of these earmarking approaches.

College Station, Texas:

4b.) Neighborhood parks are those parks providing for a variety of outdoor recreational opportunities and within convenient distances from a majority of the residences to be served thereby. The park zones established by the Parks and Recreation Department and shown on the official Parks and Recreation map for the City of College Station shall be prima facie proof that any park located therein is within such a convenient distance from any residence located therein. The primary cost of neighborhood parks should be borne by the ultimate residential property owners who, by reason of the proximity of their property to such parks, shall be the primary beneficiaries of such facilities. Therefore, the following requirements are adopted to effect the purposes stated.

4c.) To the extent that Section 4b is not applicable, the dedication requirement shall be met by a payment in lieu of land at a per-acre price set from time to time by resolution by the City Council, sufficient to acquire land and provide for adjacent streets and utilities for a neighborhood park to serve the park zone in which such development is located. Unless changed by the City Council, such per-acre price shall be computed on the basis of $225 per dwelling unit. Cash payments may be used only for acquisition or improvement of a neighborhood park located within the same zone as the development (Ord. 980, Section 16, 4E,).

Kansas City, Missouri:

Cash in lieu of land dedication. Notwithstanding anything contained in subsection (b) above, the subdivider, at the subdivider's sole option which may be elected at any time prior to approval of the preliminary plat by the plats review committee or the city plan commission based upon the election of the developer, may pay cash in lieu of dedicating open space, the subdivider shall deposit with the City Treasurer for the Parks and Recreation Acquisition and/or Development Trust Fund, prior to recording the subdivision plat, a cash payment without recourse or the right of recovery equal to the Required Parkland Dedication multiplied by the current year's price for the calendar year in which the preliminary plat is approved by the plats review committee or in the alternative the city plan commission, less a credit that any land actually dedicated for park purposes bears to the Required Parkland Dedication. Such funds shall be used for the acquisition, development or improvement of a public park generally, within one (1) mile of the periphery of the subdivision for which they were paid by the Parks and Recreation Department as authorized by the City charter (Chap. 31 Code of General Ordinances Sec. 31.31 [c]).

Mount Prospect, Illinois:

The cash contributions in lieu of park and recreation land dedication shall be held in trust by the Village or other public body designated by the Village, solely for the acquisition of park and recreation land as hereinbefore classified, which will serve the immediate or future needs of the residents of that subdivision or development or for the improvement of other existing park and recreation land which already serves such needs (Revised Development Code, 16.407-C-1).

§5.7. Credit for Private Parks

Often a developer will dedicate a park area for the exclusive use of a subdivision. In that instance a question often arises as to whether the developer should receive credit for this private dedication against the public dedication. This provision varies among cities. As a general rule, no more than fifty percent (50%) credit should be given for private recreation facilities. The developer and/or homeowner's association should also be required to provide the jurisdiction with a binding contract or agreement stipulating perpetual maintenance which meets or exceeds the minimum standards of the jurisdiction. No open land required by the zoning ordinance should be credited as private park land.

Some ordinances provide a detailed set of criteria for determining credit for private park land; others leave this to the discretion of the Park and Recreation Board and the legislative body. The following ordinance provisions illustrate the more detailed criteria.

Walnut Creek, California:

10.1.602.10. Credit for Private Recreation or Open Space. Where a substantial private park and recreational area is provided in a proposed subdivision and such space is to be privately owned and maintained by the future residents of the subdivision, partial credit, not to exceed 50%, may be given against the requirement of land dedication or payment of fees in lieu of, if the Park and Recreation Commission finds that it is in the public interest to do so and that all the following standards are met:

(a) That yards, court areas, setbacks and other open areas required to be maintained by the zoning and building ordinances and regulations shall not be included in the computation of such private open space;

(b) That the private ownership and maintenance of the open space is adequately provided for by recorded written agreement, conveyance or restrictions;

(c) That the use of the private open space is restricted for park and recreational purposes by recorded covenant, which runs with the land in favor of the future owners of property and which cannot be defeated or eliminated without the consent of the City or its successor;

(d) That the proposed private open space is reasonably adaptable for use for park and recreational purposes, taking into consideration such factors as size, shape, topography, geology, access and location;

(e) That facilities proposed for the open space are in substantial accordance with the provisions of the Recreational Element of the General Plan; and

(f) That the open space for which credit is given is a minimum of two (2) acres and provides a minimum of four (4) of the local park basic elements listed below, or a combination of such and other recreational improvements that will meet the specific recreation park needs of the future residents of the area:

Criteria List	Acres
Children's play apparatus area	.50 - .75
Landscape park-like and quiet areas	.50 - 1.00
Family picnic area	.25 - .75
Game court area	.25 - .50
Turf playfield	1.00 - 3.00
Swimming pool (42'x75') with adjacent deck and lawn areas)	.25 - .50
Recreation center building	.15 - .25

Before credit is given, the Parks and Recreation Commission shall make written findings that the above standards are met (Municipal code, Article 6, Sec. 10-1.602.10, Ord. 1603).

§5.8. Other Considerations

Plat review procedures vary according to the size of the community, the level of development activity and the complexity of the ordinance. Generally, the plat review process is either two tier, for minor subdivisions (sketch plat and final plat) and three tier for major subdivision (sketch plat, preliminary plat and final plat). The definition of minor and major is either set forth in state statute or defined in the local ordinance.

Park land should be selected at the sketch plat stage if it is to be a dedication requirement. The ordinance should state when the final dedication is to be perfected, which is usually at the time of approval of the final plat. Thus, the jurisdiction must decide on land, fee or some of both when and how or by what means the fee is to be paid. Some suggested language is:

> Procedure: At the time of approval of the tentative subdivision map or parcel map, the City shall determine the land to be dedicated, and/or fees to be paid by the subdivider. At the time of the filing of the final subdivision map, the subdivider shall dedicate the land, or pay fees, as previously determined by the City Council.[5]

Commencement of Development. The ordinance should set forth the time period for expending the fee. Construction and/or improvement of the park may be required as part of the initial infrastructure development and installation. Generally, the ordinance sets a standard, for example, that park development must begin when X percent or up to one-half of the building permits for lots in the subdivision have been taken out. Some general language would be:

> Commencement of Development: At the time of approval of the tentative subdivision map, the City Council shall specify when the development of the park or recreational facilities shall be commenced, giving highest priority to neighborhood parks.[6]

Non-residential Development. Most non-residential plats (developments) are exempt from the requirements of the park land dedication requirements. Some ordinances provide that should such land be rezoned and replatted for residential development at any time, or within a specified time, the park land dedication provisions would apply. Sometimes this is left to the discretion of the Planning Commission or the City Council.

Bloomington, Minnesota:

> (ii) Commercial, Industrial, or Other Subdivisions. As a general rule, the City shall not require park donation in commercial, industrial, or other non-residential subdivisions. In those instances, however, where the City Council deems it in the public interest to require park donation from such subdivisions, it may require dedication of an amount of land equal in value to five percent of the undeveloped land proposed to be subdivided. Said donated land shall be used only for the acquisition or development of land for parks, playgrounds, public open space, or storm water holding areas or ponds (Bloomington City Code Sec. 16.09 [B][II][ii]).

Jurisdiction Share of Adjacent Infrastructure. The proportion of adjacent infrastructure costs for which the municipality will pay can be included in the ordinance. The following illustration is from the City of Corpus Christi, Texas.

> (f) The city shall bear its portion of the cost of curbs, gutters, sidewalks and paving on any streets bounding the park in the subdivision being dedicated and shall also pay the cost of any utility extensions required to serve the park. (Ord. 15517).

In many park land reservations the jurisdiction will agree to pay at least one half or sometimes all of the adjacent infrastructure costs. Paying for all the costs may be viewed as excessive; even one-half may seem extremely generous. Where the law does not require it, such a provision is not recommended.

Severability. The severability provision is a standard last section of every statute or ordinance. In essence it declares that if any section, subsection, sentence, clause, standard, formula or provision of the statute or ordinance is held invalid, the remainder of the statute or ordinance shall not be affected by a finding of invalidity.

It is suggested, but not considered a requirement, that the following items be appended to the ordinance (or article of the subdivision code).

1. General guidelines for applying the provisions of the ordinance, with sufficient graphic illustrations.
2. A map of the service communities and/or park and recreation service zones.
3. The planning sectors of the community.
4. The major statistical areas of the community.

C. SUMMARY

A properly drafted park land dedication ordinance is one that meets several criteria.

1. The ordinance must comply with the state enabling statute and the applicable case law within that state. Further, the ordinance must serve to implement the park and recreation policies set forth in the park and recreation element of the comprehensive plan. It must be able to pass both legal and political muster, the latter often being more difficult than the former. However the ordinance is drafted, it must fit the times and be sufficiently flexible and cost effective for contemporary fast-track administration.

2. The dedication formula must be reasonable and equitable, and based on accepted planning procedures. The standard of X acres/ 1000 population seems to be the most effective in growing cities where there is a variety of special variants and/or contemporary housing types and densities. One major factor contributing to its effectiveness is that it directly relates park demand to the number of people generated by a given project. The logic is simple; it is the people who create the demand, not the number of units or the amount of land being developed. Any city contemplating the adoption of such a program should, based on their own park demand situation, consider ratios ranging from 2.5 acres to 5 acres per 1,000 people.[7]

3. The ordinance should be sensitive to current development trends, land values and roles of recreation providers within the jurisdiction. Park and recreation planners should constantly monitor park use and facility maintenance. For example, children playing in streets and vacant lots could be a sign of inadequate park resources. Vacant large parks could be viewed as excessive if they are not developed to meet the needs and demands of neighborhood residents.

4. Park and recreation needs should be assessed on a frequent and regular basis using accepted needs assessment procedures. Specific strategies to meet these needs, such as use of the school/ park concept, should be set forth in the plan.

5. Prior to drafting an ordinance a city must determine its park and recreational needs. Areas of future growth should be surveyed to determine whether school sites shall be used for public recreation. If so, agreements should be made with the school districts for such a provision.[8]

6. The ordinance should be designed to fit the needs of the city.

This cannot occur until the needs of the city are determined. Analysis will be necessary to identify current park demand, potential park sites, current land values, and the city's overall goal regarding the provision of park and recreational amenities.[9]

7. Park fees (cash-in-lieu of land) or rates should be adjusted to reflect the cost of living index and the behavior of the residential real estate market (land values) within the jurisdiction. This can insure that adequate funds are available to purchase and develop park land and recreation facilities.

CHAPTER FIVE NOTES

1. R.H. Freilich and P.S. Levi, *Model Subdivision Regulations: Text and Commentary* (Chicago: American Planning Assoc., 1975), p. 103.
2. Letter from M.T. Azeka, INFRA, p. 6.
3. "Adding Parkland To Your Community Through Mandatory Dedication" (Harrisburgh: Dept. of Community Affairs. Leisure Technical Assistance Publication, 1976), p. 8.
4. Freilich and Levi, Supra, p. 121.
5. Letter from M.T. Azeka to James Duncan, Director, Office of Land Development Services, City of Austin, Texas May 28, 1985, p. 10.
6. Ibid. p. 10.
7. Ibid. p. 14.
8. Ibid. p. 15.
9. Ibid. p. 15.

CHAPTER SIX

Problems and Opportunities
With Park Land Dedication

A. LIMITATIONS ON PARK LAND DEDICATION

§6.1. When to Use Mandatory Dedication

An excessive reliance on mandatory dedication to acquire and develop neighborhood parks is not a propitious public policy. A prudent policy should encourage the use of a panoply of tools. Selection of an acquisition procedure is based as much on the political/philosophical disposition of the community as on the statutory and constitutional basis for the procedure.

Many municipal park and recreation agencies have enjoyed good relations with developers over the years and may view mandatory dedication as excessive government intervention or regulation. Many cities take this approach, which is reasonable and understandable if they are meeting the park and recreation space needs of the citizens. There have been some dismal failures, however. Until recently, Houston, Texas experienced one of the fastest growth rates of any city in the nation, yet for years it had the lowest per capita park land acreage of any major city in the nation.[1] By contrast, Dallas, Texas has a nationally recognized park and recreation system, with park acquisition handled through procedures developed by the Dallas Park Board. Dallas opts to use reservation and purchase rather than mandatory dedication, although the latter has been held constitutional in Texas. As reported by one researcher:

> Dallas acquires parkland by several methods. The city anticipates future demand for parks in areas of new development and tries to acquire suitable land before any development begins. The effectiveness of this method directly relates to the availability of funds. The city has in the past received gifts of parkland from developers which offers good public relations and serves as a tax write-off for the developer. The city primarily tries to work

with developers on a case-by-case basis. Negotiations between the developers and the city have proven to be effective. An example would be that the developer would offer land in a flood plain for dedication and the city would ask for 10 to 15 acres more for park use. In turn the city would offer the developer such things as an increase in density or lower street standards.[2]

The actual process is one of negotiation which appears to be a successful strategy. Dallas park and planning staff seem to like the flexibility this procedure offers when working with a variety of complex development situations.

We suggest that a municipality, prior to the adoption of mandatory dedication, review (1) past history of acquiring and developing park land, (2) pace of growth, (3) attitudes of realtors and developers, (4) current land prices, (5) needs for park and recreation land and (6) prevailing attitudes and disposition of the park board, planning commission and legislative body. If mandatory dedication is legal within the state we recommend it simply because it is a tool for providing park land and recreation facilities needed to serve the new residents of the subdivision. If the law is on your side and the procedures set forth in this book are followed, there is no need to be timid or fear the use of mandatory dedication and/or cash in lieu of land if that is what is needed to assure that the basic park and recreation needs of the citizens are met.

§6.2. Size and Type of Subdivision

Many subdivision plats contain fewer than 20 development lots. A minor subdivision is often defined as a parcel subdivided into two or more development lots. Small or minor subdivisions usually do not require much in the way of new streets or other public improvements. Whether the plat is a simple lot split or small development, many ordinances exempt such plats from certain requirements of the platting ordinance.[3]

With respect to the park land dedication provisions, we suggest exempting these plats from land dedication in favor of the cash-in-lieu and/or facility/capital improvement fee. The exception would be if the plat contained land designated on the park master plan. In instances where an official park map is used, and in particular, if small plat subdivisions are the rule in the jurisdiction, we recommend a strategy whereby the jurisdiction (a) requires the right of first refusal for all designated park sites and (b) requires the cash which can be used to purchase and improve the park site.

As a general rule park land and/or cash in lieu of park land is not exacted from non-residential developments. Industrial subdivisions do not generate the need for parkland. They do, however, contribute to the overall population growth of a region. Using legislation referred to as "tax base sharing," a predominately non-residential development may be required to pay a development fee which is apportioned to jurisdictions within a designated region where the preponderance of employees live.

An exception to the general rule is offered in Bloomington, Minnesota. Under that city's ordinance, the option of imposing a land exaction on commercial and industrial subdivisions is left to the discretion of the planning commission. This is a strategy as yet untested by the courts and it appears to stretch several legal theories beyond reason.

§6.3. Neighborhood Recycling

In addition to new development there is a growing trend toward renovating or recycling older neighborhoods. This involves a gradual demographic shift from older, childless couples to younger families, either as home owners or as tenants. Cities have several powers available to guide this transition. These include preparation of special district or neighborhood plans, use of overlay zoning districts such as urban design or historic preservation districts, upzoning of vacant or recently cleared properties, and stringent housing and related code enforcement policies. Often new and old residents in such neighborhoods band together to form a neighborhood association which is chartered to work directly with city hall. Parks and playgrounds in such neighborhoods may have fallen into disrepair, may be small, built to older standards, or in a condition far below that currently in use elsewhere in the community. When such neighborhoods are recycled and reinvigorated, an improvement of the parks and recreation facilities should be an integral part of the process.

Recycling can be stimulated by the private sector, public sector, or preferably through a public/private partnership. The city, through the capital improvement program, plays a key role in this process. The jurisdiction can aid through capital improvements such as rehabilitating streets, water and sewer lines and parks and playgrounds. This can include new equipment, landscaping and the complete renovation of facilities such as restrooms and swimming pools. Funding for such renovation can come from the local general fund, general obligation bonds, other bonds, state grants, federal grants including neighborhood development grants, and private resources. Recycling of old or undeveloped neighborhoods can occur when (1) apartments are converted to condominiums or (2) an area is rezoned. In either instance, the action may trigger the imposition of park exactions.

When apartments are subdivided by legal instruments into owner-occupied units, with each owner having an easement interest in the common spaces within the facility, it may become a condominium. If state law and local ordinance require that the site (development lot) be replatted, the appropriate cash in lieu of land could be levied to pay for the park land which the population of the condominium development would require. This situation is illustrated in *Wright Development v. City of Mountain View,* 125 Cal. Rptr. 721 (Calif 1976) where a developer, who abandoned a plan to convert an apartment building into a condominium, brought action against the city to recover the subdivision fee which he paid as a precondition to approval of the subdivision map. Since the conversion never took place, the court held that the developer was entitled to the return of the subdivision fee. Had the apartment conversion proceded the fee would have been upheld.

For a variety of reasons, land zoned for low density residential often does not develop. In these instances the property may be zoned to a higher density, usually a specific use type zone, with light commercial and/or professional office space included. If the zoning is approved the existing plat must be vacated and park land dedication and capital improvement fee requirements may be imposed. Generally, if there is an adjacent park, it may be desirable to exact some land and cash so that the park space and park facilities will be adequate to serve the higher density of the new development plat. Private park and recreation credits could be invoked if necessitated and applicable.

§6.4. Planned Unit and Cluster Development

This development type, known as the "PUD," is simply a flexible form of zoning through which a developer may get more development density per unit of developable land, minimize construction costs, and provide more open space. Generally, PUDs are mixed use developments; they can contain residential, commercial and compatible industrial or high-tech research or development industry. Clustering of these uses is a design approach used to group lots in such a way as to be site responsive, require less land and less infrastructure, provide more open space and enhance the aesthetics of the development.

Park land dedication standards apply to PUDs in basically the same way as they apply to conventional subdivision plats. The PUD will normally have several distinct neighborhoods, with neighborhood schools. Depending upon the size (area) it may have junior and/or senior high schools or even community college sites. The park and recreation interest in the PUD and/or cluster is more complex than in a conventional subdivision because of several distinct characteristics: (1) the tendency to have more private recreation spaces and neighborhood facilities owned and maintained by home owner associations, (2) more trails connecting unit components, which also may serve as utility and drainage easement, and (3) more open space ranging from micro sites to boulevards, ponds, woods and other more natural areas. As Babcock notes:

> It is the nature of most PUDs to result in more common open space than

would be found in standard residential developments because clustering of dwelling units, a hallmark of a PUD, leads to substantial areas not appurtenant, so to speak, to any particular dwelling unit. This requires some device to maintain the open space (which may include a recreation building for the residents), and this need usually results in the establishment by the developer of an association of the residents which assesses each resident his or her share of the cost of management of the common areas. In some municipalities the city reserves the right to enter the premises if the open space is badly kept up in order to maintain the premises and to assess each owner for the cost of municipal maintenance.[4]

Much of the aggregate open space is not park land *per se* and should not be credited against the basic park land dedication requirement. A good deal of the non-recreation open space comes from variable zoning, irregular lot size and commons in the clusters.

The PUD approval requires a specific review and public hearing agenda. Park land interests should be identified in the preapplication conference, or the site visit, and throughout the zoning, plat review and approval process. Sites should be selected, protected and dedicated concurrently with school sites and other required dedications and/or easements. Some lands may be reserved for future purposes. Private recreation credits must be approved at this time along with the covenants and homeowner's association legal documents governing the development and maintenance of the private recreation spaces and facilities.

§6.5. Requirements Beyond the Exaction

A jurisdiction may desire park or open space land within an area which exceeds that which would be required from one or more subdivision plats. There are several ways this extra land can be acquired as part of the annexation and/or plat approval process using a procedure which is referred to as advance acquisition.

Reservation on the Land Use Map. Given statutory authority to use the official map, future park sites may be reserved for eventual purchase and/or dedication on the official map. These sites may also be delineated/designated on the future land use map of the comprehensive general plan. No development or building permits may be issued on land designated on the official map until the jurisdiction acts upon the designation within a statutory or otherwise recognized reasonable time or the lands are released from official map designation.

Right of First Refusal. Through this procedure the municipality enters into a contract with the landowner whereby the landowner agrees that when he sells the property the municipality has the first right of purchase. This contract is a right, as defined in Black's Law Dictionary as "the act of one who has by law, a right and power of having or doing something of advantage, and declines it."[5] In essence, this simply means that the owner of such designated property is only required to give the municipality the first opportunity to purchase the property at whatever price the owner asks. The municipality may wish to take an option on the property if it does not have the cash immediately available. If the municipality exercises its right of first refusal and declines to purchase the property, the lien is extinguished and the owner is free to use the land for whatever purposes are permitted or approved. Zoning *may not* be used to restrict future uses in order to depress property values in anticipation of future acquisition or condemnation by the municipality for park, recreation and/or open space purposes.

Direct Acquisition. The jurisdiction may, in accordance with applicable statutes, ordinances and regulations, expend funds to acquire park property. This action may embrace any one or a combination of the many innovative techniques developed in recent years by public and private entities active within the real estate market. Some of these strategies include:

1. purchases by a non-profit open lands trust or conservancy for eventual resale to the jurisdiction;
2. donation of the property by the owner where favorable tax treatment benefits the donor;
3. bargain sale, where the seller may realize the desired favorable tax treatment;
4. purchase by the jurisdiction and lease back for specified uses which will aid in improving the land for its eventual use for park, recreation and/or open space purposes;
5. purchase with grant of life tenancy to the surviving spouse and/or identified members of the owner's immediate family;
6. lease for park purposes with option to purchase at park land value, with lease payments applied to the reduction of the final purchase price.

§6.6. Extraterritorial Jurisdiction

In states without county zoning the question frequently arises as to what extent, if any, the municipal subdivision plat requirements can be applied within the municipality's extraterritorial jurisdiction (E.T.J.). Basically the E.T.J. is that land outside a municipal corporate boundary, up to a certain distance as defined by state statute, in which certain municipal ordinances and codes may be applied to land development and construction within subdivisions which may eventually be annexed into the corporate jurisdiction. Subdivision control ordinances, when authorized by state legislation, may regulate the subdivision of land not only within the city limits but for limited distances (1-3 miles) beyond the city limits.[6] This regulation usually applies to design and safety standards. There are no reported cases where a park land exaction imposed on a subdivision in a municipality's E.T.J. was either upheld or rejected. A municipality that imposes a park land exaction on an E.T.J. subdivision will be in virgin legal territory.

§6.7. School-Park Concept

The role of schools in providing park and recreation opportunities varies from one state and municipality to the next. In those municipalities where the school is involved in providing park and recreation areas at schools sites the relationship is called the school-park concept. Implicit in this concept is the joint sharing, between the municipality and the school, of capital and operating costs of the facility. In the context of subdivision regulations the concept is reflected in the practice of a dedication of adjoining school and park sites.

The basis for upholding mandatory dedication of land for schools is the same as that for parks, namely that the subdivider benefits financially from the exaction. Because school districts do not possess subdivision regulatory authority the municipality must impose the school land exaction. The prevailing view is that the state may authorize the municipal imposition of the school site exaction but that authority must be explicitly granted in the enabling legislation and specified in the municipal ordinance. For case law on this subject see *Midtown Properties, Inc. v. Twp. of Madison*, 172 A.2d 40 (N.J. 1961), *West Park Ave, Inc. v. Twp. of Ocean*, 224 A.2d 1 (N.J. 1966), *Krughoff v. City of Naperville*, 354 N.E.2d 489 (Ill 1976).

B. SPECIAL RESOURCES

§6.8. Sensitive Lands

These lands, which are generally classified as open space, often make up a significant percentage of the gross land area of a plat. Usually such areas are designated on the comprehensive general plan land use map or as separate overlay maps which accompany specific chapters or elements of the plan. As a general rule these areas have limited recreational potential, usually passive in nature, and should be distinguished from the generic park and recreation land required to meet the minimum standard set forth in the plan.

Critical and/or sensitive lands represent such features as ecological niches, habitats, processes, systems or areas such as community forests, watersheds or prime agricultural lands. All can contribute to a parkscape or coherent regional landscape. They may be public, private or quasi-public, and can be linked together by several legal instruments providing access and use pursuant to the characteristics of the resources, the objectives of management and the desires of the owners. Many such lands are owned by community land conservancies and trusts.

All land and water resources within the jurisdiction which exhibit any characteristics suggesting environmental limitations or severe constraints to development should be identified in the environmental inventory and analysis portion of the comprehensive general plan process. These ecological systems and processes should be delineated on appropriate maps and described and characterized using acceptable and scientifically sound procedures.

Resource protection standards governing the site development process may be found in the zoning ordinance, the subdivision platting ordinance, a separate code of overlay environmental protection ordinances or in a comprehensive development code. Some basic language is found in the subdivision regulations of *Kansas City, Missouri:*

> Sec. 31.30. Suitability of land.
> Land subject to improper drainage, or erosion, extreme topography or which, for other reasons, is unsuitable for development, shall not be platted for any use that will constitute a danger to health, safety or property destruction.
> Any proposed development within a floodplain shall be reviewed to assure that: 1) the proposal is consistent with the need to minimize flood damage; 2) public utilities and facilities are located and constructed to minimize or eliminate flood damage; and 3) adequate drainage is provided to reduce exposure to flood hazards.

These regulations address protection of resource systems such as flood hazard areas, drainageways, shorelines and storm-water retention ponds. Protection of other resource amenities can be accomplished by a variety of zoning, easement, transfer of development rights, acquisition and open space or use value taxation strategies. Without this type of express provision, such lands are not public and therefore cannot be considered as public park land, but only as common amenity open space which may buffer, protect and otherwise enhance public or private recreational spaces.

A recommended provision for a subdivision ordinance which addresses these kinds of land is as follows.

> 4.10 Preservation of Natural Features and Amenities
> (1) General.
> Existing features which would add value to residential development or to the local government as a whole, such as trees, as herein defined,

watercourses and falls, beaches, historic spots, and similar irreplaceable assets, shall be preserved in the design of the subdivision. No trees shall be removed from any subdivision nor any change of grade of the land effected until approval of the preliminary plat has been granted. All trees on the plat required shall be walled and protected against change of grade. The sketch plat shall show the number and location of existing trees, as required by these regulations and shall further indicate all those marked for retention, and the location of all proposed shade trees required along the street side of each lot as required by these regulations.[7]

Developer provided and/or protected site amenities can also include tree preservation, tree planting and the requirement of a dedicated shade tree easement or parkway as it has been designated in our older cities. Often such easements are part of a community-wide or even county or region-wide parkway system. Suggested language for such a provision follows.

(2) Shade Trees Planted by Developer
   (a) As a requirement of subdivision approval the applicant shall plant shade trees on the property of the subdivision. Such trees are to be planted within five (5) feet of the right-of-way of the roads within and abutting the subdivision, or, at the discretion of the Planning Commission, within the right-of-way of such roads. One (1) tree shall be planted for every forty (40) feet of frontage along each road unless the Planning Commission, upon recommendation of the Local Government Engineer, shall grant a waiver. Such waiver shall be granted only if there are trees growing along such right-of-way or on the abutting property which in the opinion of the Planning Commission comply with these regulations.
   (b) New trees to be provided pursuant to these regulations shall be approved by the Local Government Engineer and shall be planted in accordance with the regulations of the Local Government Engineer. Such trees shall have a minimum trunk diameter (measured twelve inches above ground level) of not less than two (2) inches. Only Oak, Honey Locust, Hard Maples, Ginkgo, or other long-lived shade trees, acceptable to the Local Government Engineer and to the Planning Commission, shall be planted.
(3) Shade Tree Easement and Dedication. The preliminary plat and final plat shall reserve an easement authorizing the local government to plant shade trees within five (5) feet of the required right-of-way of the local government. No street shall be accepted for dedication until the Local Government Engineer shall inform the Planning Commission and the Governing Body that compliance, where necessary, has been made with these regulations.[8]

Consideration of such provisions should be based on the degree of variety, character, ecological complexity and aesthetics of the indigenous community and/or regional landscape.

§6.9. Site Management

It is not uncommon for some contractors and developers to utilize environmentally damaging construction practices in the name of time and cost efficiency. A common practice is to dump trash and construction debris on the public sites within the plat. Parking and maneuvering of construction vehicles on park land can damage trees, shrubs, grass and other features as well as cause soil erosion and stream pollution. The following language, from the model subdivision regulations, addresses a part of this concern.

> (5) Debris and Waste. No cut trees, debris, earth, rocks, stones, soil, junk, rubbish, or other waste materials of any kind shall be buried in any land, or left or deposited on any lot or street at the time of the issuance of a certificate of occupancy, and removal of same shall be required prior to issuance of any certificate of occupancy on a subdivision. Nor shall any be left or deposited in any area of the subdivision at the time of expiration of the performance bond or dedication of public improvements, whichever is sooner.
>
> (6) Fencing. Each subdivider and/or development shall be required to furnish and install fences wherever the Planning Commission determines that a hazardous condition may exist. The fences shall be constructed according to standards established by the Local Government Engineer and shall be noted as to height and material on the final plat. No certificate of occupancy shall be issued until said fence improvements have been duly installed.[9]

In addition, and depending on the landscape character within a particular jurisdiction, the following provisions may be necessary to protect dedicated but undeveloped park land.

- No burrowing or excavation of top soil or earth products,
- No removal of trees for use elsewhere in the development,
- No storage of construction materials,
- No storage, parking and/or maintenance of contractor vehicles or equipment,
- No crossing the site with vehicles, including stream crossings as part of haul roads,
- No pumping of water on the park site, or water from ponds, lakes or water courses on the site for use off the park site,
- No temporary or permanent construction of overhead or underground utility lines of any kind.

The final decision on using these or other provisions should be left to the Planning Commission based on technical recommendations from the Park and Recreation Board.

C. TRENDS

§6.10. Negative Park Attitudes

Although the provision of public parks has been universally recognized as a legitimate exercise of the police power, in that it protects and enhances public health and welfare, there remain some critics. There are developers, citizens, planning commission members and judges who, for one reason or another, do not recognize the values of neighborhood parks, playfields, or other kinds of community open spaces. The reasons for these perceptions, attitudes and/or values vary considerably. Personal experiences, observations and news accounts seem to carry considerable influence in these situations.

One of the most sobering negative indictments of the value and social utility of neighborhood parks is found in *City of College Station v. Turtle Rock Corp.* 666 S.W.2d 318 (Tx 1984). In this intermediate level appellate court decision (later overturned by the Texas Supreme Court, 680 S.W.2d 802) Mr. Justic Sears wrote, "In reference to this holding, *** we note that parks are not necessarily beneficial to a community or neighborhood. Unfortunately, in some neighborhoods, parks serve as gathering places for derelicts and criminals, and are unsafe for use by law-abiding citizens. We disagree with Appellant's suggestion that neighborhood parks necessarily benefit the general public."

This reasoning could have come from experiences such as inadequate maintenance, public nuisance type activities, morally offensive activities, noise, drugs, traffic, congestion, property destruction and an overall poor physical or visual appearance of a park or playfield. Many people simply do not want an invasion of people from outside the neighborhood using a public park which they perceive to be "their neighborhood park." This feeling has prompted many developers to construct private parks which are owned and operated exclusively by the neighborhood residents through home owner's associations. This can lead to the "fortress" type cluster residential development which is appearing on the fringe of many affluent communities.

There is no easy way to prevent this negative attitude. However, if the park and recreation department is held in high esteem in the community, such practices should be fairly simple to dismiss. We recommend that all parks, especially neighborhood park and recreation facilities, be properly designed, soundly constructed, safe, attractive, adequately supervised and maintained in a professional manner.

Improper development of recreation facilities, poor facility placement within a park, scheduling and timing of high-participation and crowd-generating activities can annoy and alienate adjacent property owners and citizens. Night softball, for example, can result in problems with bright lights, noise, traffic, parking and concession litter. Lighted tennis courts, poorly located in a small neighborhood park, can disturb the use and enjoyment of adjacent private property. Aside from the nuisance like characteristics which affect enjoyment of private property, blighted parks can adversely impact property values, thereby enraging the affected parties.

§6.11. Park Linkage

Neighborhood, community, metropolitan and regional parks are all part of a jurisdiction-wide or regional open space system. Most of these natural resource facilities provide primarily passive recreation but, site compatible active recreation facilities may be developed in some instances. With many of these sites, aesthetics and protection of an ecological system are the principal reasons for prohibiting or limiting development. These types of resources do not substitute for and should not be credited for the park or recreation land needed to meet the basic needs of the residents of a particular subdivision.

An area-wide or region-wide open space system occurs by design, plan, policy, regulatory programs, public acquisition programs, private trusts and conservancies, and joint public-private ventures. Linkages to all public sites can be provided by a variety of legal instruments provided these linkages are identified on the park, recreation and open-space master plan. (See Figure 6.1). This can be viewed as a regional landscape management effort containing mixed land uses and public and private open spaces. On a regional basis the entire area may be defined as a greenline park, which offers a host of planning and management challenges as well as numerous preservation, conservation and outdoor recreation opportunities.

§6.12. Land Exchange

Many states expressly prohibit the sale or exchange of public park land. While the thought of such an act is repugnant to park and recreation professionals, there may be, under tightly controlled conditions, situations where such a land exchange may benefit the jurisdiction.

Land exchanges to round out holdings, improve parks or forests or prevent or diminish existing or potential threats to park land are frequently undertaken by federal, state, county and special district park agencies. Several potential scenarios could arise in urban environs where land exchanges and/or park land replacement may actually benefit the jurisdiction and a particular neighborhood. Depending upon how the park came to the jurisdiction park land may be sold or traded to the benefit of the jurisdiction. In many instances sentimental attachments will arise, often to the point of impeding or preventing prudent business decisions. These situations are delicate and must be handled by the Park Board, Planning Commission and

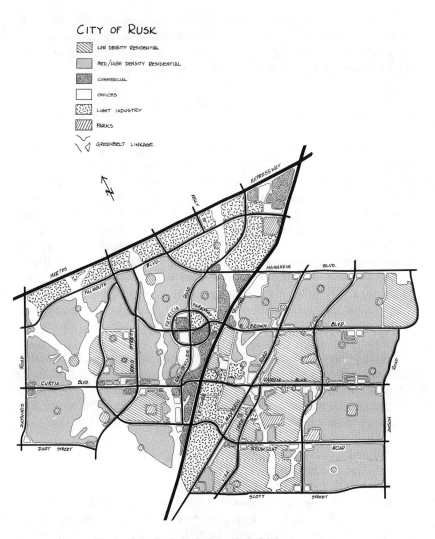

Figure 6-1. Park and Greenbelt Linkage.

legislative body with the greatest of care, precision, and understanding. Consider the following situation, where in October of 1984 the Orlando City Council voted to sell Beardall Park in downtown Orlando to developers. The one-acre mini park was to be sold for $118,000 and the developer, a large bank, was to pay the city an additional $568,000 and construct a large public play area in the heart of their office-hotel shopping complex.[10] Opponents challenged the sale, demanding that the city show "good cause" for making the sale.

Beardall Park was a gift from a prominent family which in 1984 was a small, marginally used site. The "good cause" which the city argued was the replacement of the one acre park with a 29,500 sq. ft. park in a redevelopment which would generate a considerable amount of new economic activity and tax base for the city. The $118,000 paid for the park could be used to purchase and/or improve other park land and recreation facilities within the city.

Such situations occur not only in downtown redevelopment projects, but also in neighborhood developments. When a developer pays the fair market price for the park land, agrees to replace the park land and construct a new park the jurisdiction's interest is protected. To implement this practice we suggest a legal document (contract) rather than "promises" from the developer, on the theory that the road to eternal damnation is paved with good intentions. Park and recreation administrators must be cognizant of current developments in the real estate market and be willing to negotiate the best package for the jurisdiction if such a situation arises. This is not an endorsement or suggestion for arbitrary disposal of park land, for every acre of park and open space land is a public asset. When an exchange or sale will enhance the total park estate of the community, however, the public interest is served in both the short and long run.

§6.13. Open Space through Zoning

Under this strategy open land is reserved through the zoning ordinance in accordance with rules and regulations consistent with the enabling statute and the comprehensive general plan. This procedure is used where the open space from several development lots is aggregated into a single large parcel. It is not part of the plat dedication, as discussed in Chapter 5. An example of such a provision is found in the zoning ordinance from the *City of Albuquerque, New Mexico:*

H. Detached Open Space Regulations. In the RA-1, R-D, and other zones in areas designated by the master plan as "Developing" or "Semi-Urban," required open space may be in part on lots separate from the dwellings for which the open space need not be accessible to the residents of the related dwellings, but will preserve open space which under the terms of the master plan is important to the whole community as well as to the residents of the related dwellings. The following regulations and policies apply to such detached open space:

1. The owner of the detached open space shall forfeit permanently to the City by deed or other than as specified in 4 of this subsection; if it is preferred by the land owner, the City shall accept the land in fee simple, provided the other provisions of this subsection are met. Such deed or other legal instrument shall contain specifications consistent with this subsection and shall be filed for record with the County Clerk.

2. The City may refuse to accept the offered property interest on the ground that it is not physically suitable to meet the definition of open space or the uses listed in 4. of this subsection, thus negating that given proposal for open space provision. Detached open space in an area designated by the master plan as "Developing" shall be in a location designated for low-density use or open space by a Sector Development Plan or other portion of the master plan. The City will refuse to accept the offered property interest if, according to other plans, policies, and regulations, it must be dedicated for public right-of-way, floodway, or neighborhood park.
3. The City shall ensure that the detached open space remains in the uses listed below for at least so long as the related residential development exists. When such residential development no longer exists, the City may dispose of its open space rights, but only by trading its rights for open space rights of equal value on other land.
4. Uses shall be limited to uses similar to the following, which are found by the City to be beneficial to the whole community as well as to the residents of the dwellings which caused the land to be preserved for open space.
5. If the land acquired under these provisions is owned in fee simple by the City, it may be leased to a private organization for recreational uses, but only if such uses will be open to the general public.
6. The City shall acquire and preserve open space in the general vicinity of the related dwelling which created the open space requirement, consistent with the master plan. Preferably, the open space shall be in the area covered by the same Sector Development Plan as the related dwellings, if the dwellings are covered by such a plan. Before a property interest is acquired, the Planning Director shall certify that the land in question is a desirable open space acquisition, consistent with master plan (Zoning Ordinance, Sec 40-H).

Contrast these provisions with the plat dedication requirements of the Subdivision Ordinance of the City of Albuquerque.

D. Dedications.
  1. Dedications Required.
     Dedication of land for public use or purposes may be required for the following in accordance with the appropriate City policy and/or other applicable policies:
     a. Park sites or cash in lieu thereof pursuant to the Park Dedication and Development Ordinance, Article 7-18, R.O. 1974;
     b. Streets and other access pursuant to the Long Range Major Street Plan, Section 5 of this ordinance, and/or the Development Process Manual;
     c. Drainage facilities pursuant to the Drainage Ordinance, Article 7-9, R.O. 1974, Section 5 of this ordinance, any AMAFCA Policies, and/or the Development Process Manual; and
     d. Other public infrastructure pursuant to Section 5 of this ordinance and/or the Development Process Manual.
  2. Method of Dedication.
     a. Dedication of public areas, as required by Section 5 of this ordinance, or by other City policy requirements shall be free and clear of any liens or

encumbrances and in fee simple unless:

   (1) The subdivider demonstrates that fee simple dedication is legally feasible; or

   (2) The Development Review Board and the City Attorney find that a different type of dedication better accomplishes City policy or is provided for by specific ordinance.

   b. If dedication in other than fee simple is approved, the nature of the property interest dedicated shall be clearly indicated on the plat.

   c. When parks are dedicated, a deed to the land shall be delivered to the appropriate governmental entity.

   3. Lots for Public Areas Shown in Adopted Plans.

   If a proposed public area shown on an adopted City or County plan is located in whole or in part in the area being subdivided, an appropriate lot shall be shown as reserved or dedicated for public use on the plat; unless, when asked by the subdivider, the appropriate governmental body notifies the subdivider that it does not intend to either acquire or accept the lot within a reasonable time.

   4. Acceptance of Dedications.

   The procedure for accepting dedications of public areas and improvements is specified in Sections 4.E.2.d and 6.I. of this ordinance. Within the extraterritorial planning and platting jurisdiction dedications shall be accepted by the County in accordance with its subdivision requirements (Subdivision Ordinance, Ch.7, Art. XI, Sec. 3(D)).

This type of provision may become more widespread in redeveloping areas or areas recently annexed into the jurisdiction.

§6.14. Development Impact Fees

Fast growing municipalities have increasingly attempted to place the burden of capital costs on developers. The burden is usually transferred to the developer in the form of a subdivision exaction at the time of platting or an impact fee at the time of construction. The impact fee is conceptually similar to the in-lieu fee in that both require payment for capital facilities; the time of payment is the major difference between them. Impact fees are levied in order to generate revenue to meet the capital needs necessitated by new development. The fees are levied as a facility connection charge against buildings and are normally collected when building permits are issued. Since in-lieu fees are tied to the land platting process they can only be collected at that time. In contrast, impact fees may be levied for capital facilities outside the new development and are collected when growth occurs, creating the need for new services, rather than at the time of platting. This approach creates a more flexible cost shifting tool for local government.

Initially Florida and Utah municipalities pioneered the development of impact fees but today municipalities in 39 states have adopted such fees.[11] In a 1983 study of impact fees reported in the National Tax Journal, the average fee levied was $381.00 per dwelling unit with the lowest being $25.00 and the highest being $1800.00.[12] This same study reported the impact fees for recreational services are not yet extensively used in local government, even in those states for which an express statutory delegation or sufficient judicial opinion is available.[13]

Impact fees, like subdivision exactions, raise statutory authorization and reasonableness problems. As an offshoot of the regulatory powers of local government, impact fees fall within the ambit of police power. This characterization has been critical in avoiding their classification as a tax. Although some cases have taken the position that impact fees are taxes not specifically authorized by tax legislation, most other cases uphold impact fees as a legitimate police power activity.[14]

Development fees assessed for capital construction may include park construction which is not permitted in the land dedication or cash-in-lieu option. This feature makes the fee an attractive alternative to tax increases or municipal bonding for financing new park construction or renovation projects. If the fee is to be considered, park and community planners will have to prepare explicit future development plans in advance of actual need. We can expect to see further judicial review and refinement of this concept in the next few years.

§6.15. Unified Land Development Code

The idea of folding the zoning ordinance, subdivision ordinance, related development ordinances and environmental protection regulations into a single document is not new by any means. In 1975 the American Law Institute proposed a model code to provide a more workable and streamlined land use control system for local planning bodies, legislatures and courts.[15] The code urged that any authority to limit land development should be conditioned on the drafting and approval of a local land development plan. A feature of the code was the shift from development permitted by ordinance to development authorized by permit, based on performance standards and policies within the comprehensive general plan. Hearings and rule making procedures were to be fast tracked and development orders could be used under certain conditions.[16]

Numerous variations of this code, commonly referred to as development codes, have emerged in local jurisdictions across the country. As related to the topic of this book, the principal feature of interest is the combining of elements of zoning (use regulation) with subdivision regulation (development control) within a single code. For the developer and the municipality this has accomplished several desirable results which include:

1. all proposed development must be in accordance with the comprehensive general plan;

2. zoning (use) and development (platting) are presented and reviewed within the same set of public hearings;
3. the development or application permit requests all information needed to review the case, as opposed to relying on developer submittals and the usual list of hidden agendas which surface during work sessions and public hearings;
4. the procedure can be fast tracked, thereby saving time and expense for all parties involved; and
5. the permit application can contain the standards and criteria for park land and open space dedications which must accompany both zoning and platting actions.

Breckenridge, Colorado and Fort Collins, Colorado both have implemented a form of development code system.[17] The code is used in conjunction with the comprehensive general plan. It incorporates construction standards, building and housing codes, development districts (which in most codes replace zones or zone districts), performance standards, land subdivision, development alternatives and bonuses, development orders and public deliberations and policy changes into a single document.

CHAPTER SIX NOTES

1. J.O. Simonds, *Earthscape: a Manual of Environmental Planning* (New York: McGraw-Hill Book Co., 1978), p. 279.
2. Letter from M.T. Azeka to James Duncan, Director, Office of Land Development Services, City of Austin, Texas, May 28, 1985, pp. 11-12.
3. R.H. Freilich and P.S. Levi, *Model Subdivision Regulations: Text and Commentary* (Chicago: American Planning Assoc., 1975), pp. 33, 48-49.
4. R.F. Babcock, "Zoning" in *The Practice of Local Government Planning*, ed. by F.S. So and others (Washington D.C.: International City Management Assoc., 1979), p. 435.
5. Black's Law Dictionary—4th ed (St. Paul: West Publishing Co. 1968) p. 1447.
6. E.C. Yokley, *Law of Subdivisions*, 2nd ed. (Charlottesville: The Michie Co., 1984), p. 24.
7. Freilich and Levi, Supra, pp. 101-102.
8. Ibid. p. 101.
9. Ibid. p. 81.
10. G. Blumenstyk, "Orlando Again Agrees to sell Beardell Park," *The Orlando Sentinel*, October 23, 1985, p. B-1.
11. Downing and Frank, *Recreational Impact Fees: Characteristics and Current Usage*, 36 National Tax Journal 477, 481, (1983).
12. Ibid. p. 482.
13. Ibid. p. 488.
14. *Hartman v. Aurora Sanitary Dist.*, 177 N.E.2d 214 (Ill 1961); *Home Builders Ass'n of Greater Salt Lake v. Provo City*, 503 P.2d 451 (Utah 1972); *Contractors*

and Builders Ass'n of Pinellas County v. City of Dunedin, 329 So.2d 314 (Fla 1976).

15. A. Dunham, *A Model Land Development Code,* (Philadelphia: The American Law Institute 1975).

16. Ibid pp. 81-109.

17. Chapter 21, Breckenridge Development Code Ordinance No. 2, Series 1978, Town of Breckenridge, Colorado. and G. Delsohn, "Fort Collins" *Planning* Vol. 5 No. 10 (October 1985) pp. 25-26.

APPENDIX A
Park Land Dedication Cases by State

Alabama:
City of Montgomery v. Crosslands Land Co., 355 So.2d 363 (1978), holding that in the absence of specific statutory authority, the city had no power to impose a fee in lieu of land exaction.

Arkansas:
City of Fayetteville v. IBI, Inc., 659 S.W.2d 505 (1983) invalidating the city's fee in lieu of land exaction because it did not relate to the needs identified in the park plan.

California:
Kebler v. City of Upland, 318 P.2d 361 (1957), invalidating a $30.00 per lot park fee because the funds could be used anywhere in the city. Associated Home Bldrs. of Greater E. Bay, Inc. v. Walnut Creek, 484 P.2d 606 (1971). Codding Enterprises v. City of Merced, 116 Cal. Rptr. 730 (1974), applying park exaction to split lots of less than five acres. Wright Dev. Co. v. City of Mt. View, 125 Cal. Rptr. 723 (1975), requiring the city to refund the park fee to the developer because the project was never started. Norsco Enterprises v. City of Fremont, 126 Cal. Rptr. 659 (1976), applying the dedication rule to a conversion of apartments to condominiums. Hirsch v. City of Mt. View, 134 Cal. Rptr. 519 (1976), affirming the city's charter authority to impose a park fee. Trent Meredith, Inc. v. City of Oxnard, 170 Cal. Rptr. 685, (1981), relying on the concept of park fees to sustain a fee levied upon a developer to relieve overcrowding in a neighborhood school.

Colorado:
City of Colorado Springs v. Kitty Hawk Dev. Corp., 392 P.2d 467 (1964), upheld a park fee as condition for annexation in the city.

Connecticut:
Aunt Hack Ridge Est. Inc. v. Planning Comm'n of Danbury, 273 A.2d 880 (1970), sustaining a park land exaction as a condition of subdivision plat approval.

Florida:
Admiral Development Corp. v. City of Maitland, 267 So.2d 860 (1972) invalidated a five percent park land requirement as without statutory or home rule authorization. Broward County v. Janis Dev. Corp. 311 So.2d 371 (1975), invalidating a $200 per dwelling unit park fee because the money could be spent for any purpose anywhere in the county. Hollywood Inc. v. Broward County, 431 So.2d 606 (1983), sustaining a county ordinance requiring an exaction of three acres of park land for every 1000 residents. Town of Longboat Key v. Lands end, Ltd., 433 So.2d (1983), sustaining five acres per 1000 park land dedication formula.

Georgia:
Smith v. Gwinnett County, 286 S.E.2d 739 (1982), distinguishing between reservation and dedication of land on a subdivision plat wherein the court found the county did not accept the offers of dedication.

Illinois:
Pioneer Trust and Sav. Bank v. Village of Mount Prospect, 176 N.E.2d 799 (1961), established the specifically and uniquely attributable test. Krughoff v. City of Naperville, 354 N.E.2d 489 (1976), sustaining park land formula of 5.5 acres per 1000 population as within home-rule authority and not unreasonable.

Kansas:
Coronado Dev. Co. v. City of McPherson, 368 P.2d 51 (1962), holding that city lacked statutory authority to require a developer to pay a fee of 10 percent of the appraised value of platted area to be used for parks and recreation.

Michigan:
Ridgemont Dev. Co. v. City of East Detroit, 100 N.W.2d 301 (1960), invalidating a park land exaction as a condition of plat approval because the city lacked the statutory authority to impose the exaction. Gorden v. Village of Wayne, 121 N.W.2d 823 (1961), village without authority to require a subdivider to donate cash or property for park purposes as a condition to the approval of the subdivision plan.

Minnesota:
Collis v. City of Bloomington, 246 N.W.2d 19 (1976), sustaining the constitutionality of park-land dedication statute and the city-ordinance requirement that up to 10 percent of the development area be dedicated for public parks.

Missouri:
Home Bldrs. Ass'n of Greater Kansas City v. City of Kansas City, 555

S.W.2d 832 (1977), sustaining a park dedication formula of four acres of land per 100 living units within a subdivision.

Montana:
Billings Property Inc. v. Yellowstone Co. 394 P.2d 182 (1964), upholding the validity of a statute authority municipalities to impose park-land dedication exactions.

New Hampshire:
Patenaude v. Town of Merideth, 392 A.2d 582 (1978). J.E.D. Assoc. Inc. v. Town of Atkinson, 432 A.2d 12 (1981), invalidating a seven and one-half percent of subdivision acreage for parks as arbitrary and unreasonable.

New Jersey:
Levin v. Livingston Twp. 173 A.2d 391 (1961). 181 Inc. v. Salem County Plan. Bd. 336 A.2d 501 (1975).

New Mexico:
Sanchez v. City of Santa Fe, 481 P.2d 401 (1971), invalidating a park fee of $50.00 per lot because the fee was not authorized by statute and was in the nature of a tax.

New York:
In re Lake Secor Dev. Co. 255 N.Y.S. 853 (1932). Jenad Inc. v. Village of Scarsdale, 218 N.E.2d 673 (1966), sustaining a park land and fee exaction of $250 per lot as with the authority of the city. East Neck Estates Ltd. v. Luchsinger, 305 N.Y.S.2d 922 (1969), invalidating a required park dedication of valuable shore frontage where the value of the land to be dedicated approximated one third of the purchase price of the entire tract to be subdivided. Riegent Apts. Corp. v. Planning Bd. of Clarkston, 441 N.E.2d 1076 (1982), affirming the authority of town to impose park land and fee exactions as a condition of approving subdivision plats but rejecting the authority to impose the requirement for site plans. Kambi v. Planning Bd of Yorktown, 452 N.E.2d 1193 (1983), invalidating as unreasonable a park land dedication requirement that 40 percent of the development be dedicated as a park.

North Carolina:
Messer v. Town of Chapel Hill, 297 S.E.2d 632 (1982), sustaining park exaction ordinance as within scope of statutory powers given to city.

Oregon:
Haugen v. Gleason, 359 P.2d 108 (1961), invalidating a fee of $37.50 per lot to be used for land acquisition as beyond statutory authority.

Rhode Island:
Frank Ansuini Inc. v. City of Cranston, 264 A.2d 910 (1970), invalidating a park land requirement of seven percent of the total development as arbitrary and constitutionally invalid.

Texas:
Berg Development v. City of Missouri City, 603 S.W.2d 273 (1980), overruled by City of College Station v. Turtle Rock Corp.; 680 S.W.2d 802 (1984), sustaining the statutory authority of the city's park dedication ordinance and finding that the formula of one acre per 133 dwelling units was not *per se* unreasonable.

Utah:
Call v. City of West Jordan, 606 P.2d 217 (1979), sustaining a park exaction of seven percent of the development as within the scope of powers granted to the city by the legislature. On rehearing, 614 P.2d 1257 (1980), the 7 percent requirement was held not to be unreasonable on its face.

Virginia:
National Realty Corp. v. City of Virginia Beach, 163 S.E.2d 154 (1968), invalidating as without statutory authority a $25.00 per lot fee.

Washington:
Hillis Homes v. Snohomish County, 650 P.2d 193 (1982), invalidating a park fee of $250 per lot as a condition to plat approval on the basis that the fee was a tax not expressly authorized by the legislation.

Wisconsin:
Jordan v. Village of Menomonee Falls, 137 N.W.2d 442 (1965), sustaining an ordinance requiring a $200 per lot fee for park purposes. City of Mequon v. Lake Estates Co. 193 N.W.2d 912 (1971), sustaining a fee of $80 per lot in a subdivision for park purposes.

Wyoming:
Coulter v. City of Rawlins, 662 P.2d 888 (1983), sustaining a park exaction formula of six acres per 1000 persons as within the scope of powers granted by state enabling legislation.

APPENDIX B

State Enabling Acts

PLANNING	SUBDIVISION CONTROLS	PARK EXACTIONS
Alabama: Code of Ala §§11-52-1 et seq	§§11-52-30 et seq	
Alaska: Ala Code §29.33	§§40.15.010 et seq	
Arizona: Ariz Rev Stat §§9-463 et seq	9-463.03	§9-463.04
Arkansas: Ark Stat §§19-2826 et seq	§19-2829 (c)	§19-2829
California: Govt Code §§65100 et seq	§§66410 et seq	§66477
Colorado: Colo Rev Stat §§31-23-201 et seq	§§31-23-214 et seq	§30-28-133(4a)
Connecticut: Conn Gen Stat §§8-18 et seq	§§8-25 et seq	§8-26
Delaware: Del Code Ann Tit 22, §701 et seq		
Florida: Fla Stat Ann§§163.160 et seq	§§163.260 et seq	§177.081
Georgia: Code of Geo §§69-801 et seq	§§69-1214 et seq	
Hawaii: Haw Rev Stat §§46-5 et seq	§§46-5 et seq	§46-6
Idaho: Idaho Code §§67-6501 et seq	§§67-6513c&50-1301	
Illinois: Ill Rev Stat Ch 24, §§11-12-4 et seq	Ch 24, §11-12-8	
Indiana: Burns Ind Code §§36-7-4-100 et seq	§36-7-3-2	§53-747
Iowa: Iowa Code Ann §§409.1 et seq	§§409.1 et seq	§409.4-5
Kansas: Kan Stat Ann §§12-701 et seq	§12-705	§12-705
Kentucky: Ken Rev Stat §§100.111 et seq	§§100.273 et seq	§§100.273 et seq
Louisiana: La Stat Ann §§33.101 et seq	§§33.112 et seq	
Maine: Me Rev Stat Tit 30, §4511	Tit 30, §4956	
Maryland: Md Code Ann Art 66B, §§3.01 et seq	Art 66B, §5.01 et seq	
Massachusetts: Mass Ann L Ch 41, §70 et seq	Ch 41, §81K to 81GG	§81Q
Michigan: MSA §§5.2991 et seq	26.430(101) et seq	
Minnesota: MSA §§462.351 et seq	§462.358	§462.358
Mississippi: Miss Code §§17-1-1 et seq	§21-19-63	
Missouri: Mo Ann Stat §§89.300 et seq	§§445.010 et seq	
Montana: Mont Rev Code §§76-1-106 et seq	§§76-3-101 et seq	§76-3-606
Nebraska: Neb Rev Stat §§18-1301 et seq	§§14-115 et seq	
Nevada: Nev Rev Stat §§268.100 et seq	§§278.320 et seq	1983, Ch 532, P. 1425
New Hampshire: NH Rev Stat §§36-1 et seq	§36-19	§36-21
New Jersey: NJ Stat Ann §§40:55D-1 et seq	§§40:55D-37 et seq	
New Mexico: NM Stat §§3-19-1 et seq	§§3-20-1 et seq	
New York: NY Gen Mun L §§234 et seq	§§234 et seq	§277, §7-730
N. Carolina: Gen Stat NC §§160A-360 et seq	§§160A-371 et seq	§160A-372
N. Dakota: ND Cent Code §§40-48-02 et seq	§§40-48-18 et seq	
Ohio: Ohio Rev Code §§713.01 et seq	§§711.001 et seq	
Oklahoma: Okla Stat Ann Tit 11, §45.101	§§47-113 et seq	
Oregon: Ore Rev Stat §§227.010 et seq	§§92.010 et seq	
Pennsylvania: Pa Stat Ann Tit 53, §10101 et seq	Tit 53, §§10503 et seq	
Rhode Island: Gen L RI §§45-22-1 et seq	§§45-23-1 et seq	§45-23-10
S. Carolina: Code of L of SC §5-23-490	§§5-23-600 et seq	
S. Dakota: SD Comp L §§11-6-3 et seq	§11-6-26	
Tennessee: Tenn Code Ann §§13-4-101 et seq	§§13-4-301 et seq	
Texas: Tax Civ Stat Art 974a	Art 974a	
Utah: Utah Code Ann §§10-9-19 et seq	§§10-9-25 et seq	§57-5-4
Vermont: Vt Stat Ann §§4321 et seq	§§4413 et seq	
Virginia: Code of Va §§15.1-427 et seq	§§15.1-465 et seq	
Washington: Wash Rev Code §§35.63.010 et seq	§§58.17.010 et seq	§58.16.110
W. Virginia: W Va Code §§8-24-1 et seq	§§8-24-28 et seq	
Wisconsin: Wis Stat Ann §62.23	§§236.01 et seq	
Wyoming: Wyo Stat Ann §§15-1-502 et seq	§34-12-101	

APPENDIX C

Typical Subdivision Control Ordinance

AN ORDINANCE REGULATING THE SUBDIVISION OF LAND IN THE CITY OF . . ., REQUIRING AND REGULATING THE PREPARATION AND PRESENTATION OF PRELIMINARY AND FINAL PLANS FOR SUCH PURPOSE; ESTABLISHING MINIMUM SUBDIVISION DESIGN STANDARDS; PROVIDING MINIMUM IMPROVEMENTS TO BE MADE OR GUARANTEED TO BE MADE BY THE SUBDIVIDER; SETTING FORTH THE PROCEDURE TO BE FOLLOWED BY THE . . . PLANNING COMMISSION IN APPLYING THESE RULES, REGULATIONS AND STANDARDS; AND PRESCRIBING PENALTIES FOR THE VIOLATION OF ITS PROVISIONS.

BE IT ORDAINED BY THE BOARD OF COMMISSIONERS OF THE CITY OF . . .

SECTION 1. SHORT TITLE.

This Ordinance shall be known, and may be cited, as The Subdivision Ordinance of the City of . . ..

SECTION 2. INTERPRETATION AND PURPOSE.

In their interpretation and application the provisions of this Ordinance shall be held to be the minimum requirements adopted for the public health, safety and welfare. To protect the public, among other purposes, such provisions are intended to provide for permanently wholesome community environments, adequate municipal services and safe streets.

SECTION 3. APPROVING AGENCY.

In accordance with the provisions of Chapters . . . and . . ., Public Acts of . . ., the provisions of this Ordinance shall be administered by the . . . Planning Commission.

SECTION 4. DEFINITIONS.

For the purpose of this Ordinance, words and terms are defined as follows:

1. *Subdivision:* The division of a tract or parcel of land into two or more lots, sites, or other divisions for the purpose, whether immediate or future, of sale or building development, and includes resubdivision and, when appropriate to the context, relates to the process of subdividing or to the land or area subdivided.

2. *Plat:* The map, drawing, or chart on which the subdivider's plan of subdivision is presented and which he submits for approval and intends in final form to record; it includes plat, plan, plot and replot.

3. *Planning Commission:* The . . . Planning Commission, its Board of Commissioners, Officers or Staff.

4. *City Commission:* The Board of Commissioners of the City of . . ..

5. *City Engineer:* The regularly appointed person serving in the capacity of City Engineer appointed and functioning as provided in the . . . City Code or his authorized representative acting in his absence.

6. *Traffic Engineer:* The person duly appointed and qualified as Traffic Engineer for the City of . . ..

7. *Master Plan:* The comprehensive plan of the City of . . . approved by the Planning Commission and adopted by the City Commission which indicates the general locations recommended for functional classes of public works, places, structures, streets, parks, public buildings, playgrounds, etc.

8. *Official Map:* The map on which the planned locations, particularly the streets, are indicated with detail and exactness so as to function as the basis for property acquisition or building restriction.

9. *Zoning Ordinance:* The . . . Zoning Ordinance No . . . of . . ., 19 . . ., as amended.

10. *Street:* A Public or private way, provided for the accommodation of vehicular traffic, or as a means of access to property, and includes streets, avenues, boulevards, roads, lanes, alleys, or other ways.

11. *Main Thoroughfare:* A street designated as a Major Street on the Master Plan or on the Official Major City Street Plan.

12. *Secondary Thoroughfare:* Any highway, thoroughfare, or street other than a Main Thoroughfare.
13. *Local Service Street:* A street designated to accommodate local traffic, the major portion of which originates along the street itself.
14. *Building Line:* A line on a plat indicating the limit upon which buildings or structures may be erected.
15. *Lot Width:* The distance between side lot lines measures at the building line, as set forth in the Zoning Ordinance, parallel to the street line on which the lot fronts.

SECTION 5. LIMITS OF APPLICATION.

These Subdivision Regulations will apply within the corporate limits of the City of . . ., and to such subdivisions in the area outside the corporate limits over which the City now has or may hereafter have jurisdiction under the laws of the State of . . ..

SECTION 6. PROCEDURE.
1. *General:* Application by the owner or his authorized representative for approval of a plat of subdivision shall be made in writing to the City Engineer.
2. *Preliminary Plat:*
(a) The written application shall be accompanied by three copies of the Preliminary Plat for the subdivision of the land. The plan of subdivision shall be such as to meet, at least, the minimum requirements of this Ordinance and of the minimum standards of design herein. The Plat shall comply with the provisions, contain the information, and be accompanied by the material required by the standards adopted under this Ordinance.
(b) Previous to the submission of a Preliminary Plat, subdividers are invited to submit to the Planning Commission preliminary studies or sketches which may be helpful in discussing the preparation of the Preliminary Plat.
3. *Tentative Approval:*
(a) The subdivider shall submit to the Planning Commission three (3) copies of his preliminary plat. The Planning Commission will review the preliminary plat in conjunction with the City Engineer and the City Traffic Engineer. The Planning Commission shall, within (30) days, pass on the preliminary plat as submitted or as modified and shall express tentative approval in writing or shall express disapproval in writing with the reasons therefor.
(b) If such action be one of tentative approval, such approval shall not constitute a final acceptance of the plat, but shall be deemed merely an expression of approval of the layout submitted on the Preliminary

Plat. Approval of the Final Plat for record will be considered only after the requirements outlined herein under Section 10 shall have been fulfilled.

4. *Final Plat:*

The final or record subdivision plat shall be prepared and submitted to the Planning Commission in six (6) copies in the form of reproductions satisfactory to the Planning Commission, accurate as to scale and dimension, by the owner of the property or his authorized representative. It shall be submitted within one (1) year after the approval of the Preliminary Plat; otherwise, the approval of the Preliminary Plat shall become null and void unless an extension of time is applied for and the extension is granted by the Planning Commission. The Final Plat shall show the same layout and arrangement as that shown on the Preliminary Plat which was tentatively approved by the Planning Commission. The Final Plat shall comply with the provisions and shall contain the complete data and information required by the standards adopted and described herein, and shall be accompanied by such other data or materials as are described in Section 7 hereof. Three (3) reproductions of all final or record plats, and of the index sheet, if any, shall be furnished. The Final Plat shall be approved by the Planning Commission, such approval to be entered in writing on the Plat by the Secretary of the Commission.

5. *Endorsements:*

The Final Plat shall, where applicable, show the endorsements, dedications and certificates which have been adopted as standards and which are described herein.

SECTION 7. GENERAL REQUIREMENTS.

1. *Relief From Requirements:*

The following shall be considered as minimum requirements, and shall be varied by the Planning Commission only where practical difficulty or unnecessary hardship would be caused by their enforcement. The Planning Commission will permit a variation only where it can be done in such a way as to grant relief and at the same time protect the general interest. All such variations, and the reasons therefor, shall be noted in writing in the records of the Planning Commission.

2. *Conformity to Official Plan or Map:*

Subdivisions shall be in harmony with the master plan of . . . County and the City of . . ., and with the official map of the said county and city.

3. *Relation to Adjoining Street Systems:*

(a) Insofar as the master plan or official map does not indicate the size, location, direction and extent of a street, and subject to the regulations hereinafter specified regarding definite minimum widths, the arrangement of streets in a subdivision shall provide for the continuation of the principal streets existing in the adjoining subdivisions, or of their proper projection when adjoining property is not subdivided, and shall be of a width at least as great as that of such existing streets, except that where, in the opinion of the Planning Commission, topographical or other conditions make such continuance or conformity impracticable, the Planning Commission may approve a variation from this requirement.

(b) In cases where the Planning Commission itself prepares and adopts a plan or plat of a neighborhood or area of which the subdivision is a part and this plan or plat provides coordinations with the street system of the county or city different from that of said continuations or projections of existing streets required above, the Planning Commission may approve a subdivider's plat which conforms to such neighborhood plat or plan of the Planning Commission.

(c) Where the plat submitted covers only a part of the subdivider's tract, a sketch of the proposed future street system of that unsubmitted part, shall be furnished and the street system of the part submitted shall be considered in the light of adjustments and connections with the street system of the part not submitted.

4. *Access:*
The subdividing of the land shall be such as to provide each lot, by means of either a public street or way of permanent easement, with satisfactory access to an existing public highway, street, or to a thoroughfare as shown on the official map or the master plan.

5. *Conformity to Design Standards of the Commission:*
Subdivisions shall conform in all details to the standards of design adopted herein for street widths, street grades, street intersections, street names, easements, block lengths and widths, lot sizes, lot arrangements, building restrictions, tree planting, public open spaces, and other design standards on file at the office of the City Engineer and the Planning Commission and described herein.

6. *Monuments:*
Monuments shall be placed at all block corners, angle points, points of curves in streets, and at such intermediate points as shall be required by the City Engineer, or at related points approved by the City Engineer. Monuments shall consist of iron rods or pins at least one-half inch in diameter by two feet (2') long, set in concrete at least six inches (6") in diameter by thirty inches (30") deep, or otherwise as approved by the City Engineer.

7. *Utilities:*
Where a plat is made up of lots less than one acre in size, the City

Engineer shall require the installation of a central water system and a central sanitary sewer system, or other satisfactory sewage disposal arrangements, and provide an adequate storm sewer system or dedicate right-of-way for adequate surface storm water disposal facilities, according to the standards and specifications prescribed by the City Engineer, and in cases where connections are made to the water and sewer systems serving the City of . . ., according to standards and specifications prescribed by the City Engineer.

SECTION 8. MINIMUM STANDARDS OF DESIGN.

1. *General Requirements:*

The subdivision layouts shall meet the general requirements specified in Sections 7, 9 and 10 hereof. All street and road work shall be approved by the City Engineer.

2. *Street Widths:*

(a) The minimum width of right-of-way for main thoroughfares shall be as specified in the Major Street Plan of the city, or, where not so specified, the minimum width shall be whatever may be deemed best or necessary by the Planning Commission for the future territory in which the plat is located, except that the minimum dedicated width shall not ordinarily be less than fifty feet (50'). These widths shall be measures from lot line to lot line. In cases where the topography or other conditions make a street of the required minimum width impracticable, or inadvisable, the Planning Commission may modify the above requirements. A half street along adjoining property may be approved and should there be a half street dedicated and accepted in an adjoining plat along the boundary of this plat, the other half of said street or alley necessary to make complete such street or alley, shall be dedicated.

(b) All roadways shall have a graded width equal to the full width of the street.

(c) All roadways shall have a minimum surface width of thirty feet (30').

(d) All roadways shall have a minimum compacted surface thickness of six inches (6") and of a satisfactory material.

(e) All roadways shall have a curb.

(f) All roadways shall have adequate drainage structures with inlet and outlet ditches. The clearance between inside of all head walls of drainage structures shall be equal to the width of the street. Drainage areas shall be shown for all drainage structures and drainage ditches.

3. *Street Names:*

Extensions of existing streets shall be named the same as streets of which they are extensions. No names of new streets or plats submitted shall be duplicates of present names of streets or plats within that portion of . . . County outside of the limits of municipal corporations and the metropolitan area of . . ..

4. *Grade of Streets:*

Street grades shall be not less than one-half of one percent at the gutter, and not more than the City Engineer shall determine. Grades shall be ordinarily not more than six percent for main thoroughfares and ten percent for minor streets, except that a variation from these grades may be permitted by the City Engineer where advisable to adjust to topographical conditions.

5. *Dead End Streets:*

Streets designed to have one end permanently closed (cul de sacs) shall be provided at the closed end with a turnaround roadway having a minimum radius for the outside curb of at least thirty-five feet (35'), and a minimum radius of forty-five feet (45') to the property lines.

6. *Intersection Angles:*

As far as practicable, acute angles between streets at their intersections are to be avoided. Where a deflection angle of more than ten (10) degrees in a street line occurs at any point between two intersecting streets a curve of reasonably long radius is to be introduced.

7. *Rounding Street Corners:*

Whenever necessary to permit the construction of curbs having a reasonable radius at street corners, without curtailing the sidewalk to less than the normal width, the property line at such street corners shall be rounded or otherwise set back sufficiently to permit such construction. Normally the radius of the curb or edge of roadway at street intersections shall not be less than twenty feet (20') for local service streets and twenty-five feet (25') for secondary or main streets and thoroughfares. Larger radius may be required by the City Engineer or the Traffic Engineer when, in his opinion, such design is advisable.

8. *Easements:*

Except where alleys of not less than twenty feet (20') are dedicated, the Planning Commission may require easements not exceeding six feet (6') on each side of all rear lot lines, and on side lot lines where necessary or in the opinion of the Planning Commission advisable, for poles, wires, conduits, storm and sanitary sewers, gas, water and heat mains or other utility lines. Easements of the same or greater width may be required along the lines of or across lots where necessary for the extension of the existing or planned utilities.

9. *Block Lengths:*

In blocks over one thousand feet (1,000') in length the City Engineer may require at or near the middle of the block a public crosswalk for foot traffic, having a right-of-way of not less than fifteen feet (15') in width. Blocks of less than three hundred feet (300') or more than six hundred feet (600') are discouraged but may be approved where circumstances warrant.

10. *Block Widths:*

The widths of blocks preferably shall be such as to allow for two tiers of lots, unless exceptional conditions are, in the opinion of the City Engineer, such as to render this requirement undesirable.

11. *Lot Arrangements:*

In all quadrangular lots and, so far as practical, all other lots, the side lines shall be at right angles to straight street lines or radical to curved street lines. Arrangements placing adjacent lots at right angles to one another shall be avoided where practicable.

12. *Lot Sizes:*

The minimum dimension for residential lots shall be sixty feet (60') for width measured at the building line, and in no case shall a residence lot contain less than nine thousand (9,000) square feet. There shall be no division or subdivision of platted lots that will result in a reduction in size of any of the platted lots involved in the re-subdivision below this area. Corner lots shall have such extra width as will permit the establishment of a building line of not less than that required by the Height and Area Regulations of the . . . Zoning Ordinance. The minimum depth of all residential lots shall be one hundred and twenty-five feet (125').

13. *Building Lines and Restrictions:*

Building set back lines of minimum distance as required by Height and Area Regulations of the . . . Zoning Ordinance shall be established back of the front lot lines of all lots. Between said building set back lines and the dedicated street lines no buildings or structures shall be erected, provided that this restriction shall not apply to or preclude the erection of a pergola or open summer house.

14. *Tree Planting:*

The planting of street trees is optional with the subdivider, but if done, planting must receive the City Engineer's approval before planting of street trees is begun.

15. *Public Open Spaces:*

INSERT PARK DEDICATION PROVISIONS HERE

SECTION 9. PRELIMINARY PLAT STANDARDS.

1. *Scale:*

The scale of the preliminary plat is optional but shall not be smaller than one hundred feet (100') to one inch (1").

2. *Information to Be Shown:*
The preliminary report shall show:
(a) The location of then existing property lines, streets, buildings, water courses, railroads, utilities and other similar features.
(b) The names, location, widths, and other dimensions of proposed streets, alleys, easements, parks and other open spaces, reservations, lot lines, building lines and utilities.
(c) The approximate location of existing sewers and water mains, culverts and drain pipes, proposed to be used on the property to be subdivided, and invert elevations of sewers at points of proposed connections, grade and elevation of all drainage ditches and area to be drained.
(d) The title under which the proposed subdivision is to be recorded, with the names and addresses of the owner and the technical author of the plan; and a notation stating the acreage.
(e) The names of subdivisions immediately adjacent; also the location and names of adjacent streets and other public spaces on immediately adjoining properties.
(f) Contours at any vertical interval deemed sufficient by the City Engineer to explain the layout and design of all or details of the subdivision. Elevations shall be marked on such contours based on a datum plane approved by the City Engineer.
(g) Date, north point, and scale.
(h) The preliminary plat shall be accompanied by street profiles showing existing ground surface and proposed street grades, including extensions for a reasonable distance beyond the limits of the proposed subdivision; typical cross-sections of the proposed grading, roadway and sidewalk; and preliminary plan of proposed sanitary and storm water sewers with grades and sizes indicated. All elevations shall be based on a datum plane approved by the City Engineer.
(i) All parcels of land proposed to be dedicated to public use and the conditions of such dedication, if any.
(j) The preliminary plat also shall be accompanied by a plan indicating the use of the lots proposed by the subdivider whether for one-family dwellings, multi-family housing, business or industrial purposes; and documents or copies shall be submitted of the proposed instruments whereby the use, building line, open space and other restrictions are proposed by the subdivider to be imposed. Proposed uses must be in accord with the use provisions of the . . . Zoning Ordinance.

SECTION 10. FINAL PLAT STANDARDS AND FORMS.
1. *Drafting Standards:*
The final plat shall be drawn on sheets of not more than twenty-two

inches (22") wide by thirty-three (33") long, to a scale of not less than one hundred feet (100') to an inch (unless the Planning Commission permits a lesser scale); Provided that when more than one sheet is required, an index sheet of the same size shall be filed showing the entire subdivision at a scale to fit a single sheet with block and lot numbers indicated.

2. *Data Required:*

The final plat shall comply with and shall contain the data specified in the following:

(a) The boundary lines of all proposed streets or other ways or easements and other open spaces intended to be dedicated for public use or granted for use of inhabitants of the subdivision; lines of all adjoining streets and boundary lines of all proposed lots.

(b) (1) The boundary of the subdivided tract, with bearings and distances marked thereon. Such boundary shall be determined by survey in the field which shall be balanced, closed and referenced to adjoining streets or subdivisions in a manner satisfactory to the City Engineer, and certified to be correct by a qualified Engineer or Surveyor. (2) The length of all straight lines, radii, and arc distances; central angles on all curves, deflection angles between tangents, along the property lines of each street. All dimensions along the line of each lot, with the bearings or angles of intersection which they make with each other, or both, and any other data necessary for the location of any lot line in the field; the location of all building lines proposed by the subdivider. All lengths shall be the nearest one-hundredth of a foot, United States Standard Measures. If more convenient, bearings may be used instead of angles.

(c) The locations and plane coordinates of all required monuments (see Sections 7, 5, above) and all adjoining street intersections to the nearest one-hundredth of a foot and referred to a true (reference) meridian and to a point of origin approved by the City Engineer, such true meridian and plane coordinates being the basis also for all bearings and lengths shown on the plat. If the City has adopted an official plane coordinate system, the plane coordinates of the monuments shall be based upon such official system, by means of traverse surveys connecting the subdivision surveys with the control survey monuments of the official coordinate system. Such connecting traverse ties shall be made from at least two different points, if possible, and preferably on opposite sides of the subdivision. The accuracy of the connecting traverse shall be at least 1:10,000. An abstract of the field notes and computations therefore shall accompany the Final Plat filed with the City Engineer, showing complete details of the connecting traverses.

(d) The names of all streets or ways of the subdivision; the names of all adjoining streets or ways. The names of all subdivisions immediately adjacent, or when adjoining property is not a recorded subdivision, the name of the owners thereof; and the book and page number of the public records where adjoining subdivisions or tracts are recorded.

(e) Date, title, legend, north point, and scale. The title shall include the name of the subdivision under which it is to be recorded. The north point should indicate true north for the area, as well as the plane coordinate north in case this is different from true north. Explanatory notes should give the origin, and longitude of the reference meridian, of the plan coordinate system. The legend will show the various lines (solid, dotted, or dashed) and other symbols used with explanations thereof.

(f) All forms such as endorsements, dedications and certificates required to be shown on the plat, as described in Section 6.

(g) The Final Plat shall be accompanied by profiles of streets showing grades approved by the City Engineer. Such profiles shall be drawn to City standard scales and elevations shall be based on a datum plane approved by the City Engineer.

SECTION 11. ENDORSEMENTS AND ACCOMPANYING MATERIAL.

1. The Final Plat, where applicable, shall show the following endorsements, dedications and certificates:

   (a) Certificate of title showing the ownership of the land to be in the subdivider, or his principal, or other applicant for approval.

   (b) Certificate of dedication of streets, alleys or other public spaces by signature of the owner or owners. Said signatures must be properly acknowledged and witnessed.

   (c) Certificate by competent authority that there are no incumbrances on any lands dedicated to the public.

   (d) Description of boundary survey.

   (e) Space and form for notation of plat volume and page number and date of recording in County Register of Deeds Office.

   (f) Any other forms, endorsements, and certificates as may, in special cases, be determined by the City Engineer.

2. All forms (such as endorsements, dedications, and certificates, in so far as required to be entered on the plats) shall be in accordance with the forms adopted by the Planning Commission and described below; and, except where otherwise required or permitted, shall be signed by the owner of the property. The duplicate and triplicate of the Final Plat shall contain all signatures, endorsements, dedications and certificates, and shall be left with the Planning Commission for its files or transmission to other departments. Where a plat is filed in multi-

ple sheets all signatures, endorsements, dedications and certificates shall appear on each sheet.

SECTION 12. Developments Required Before Final Approval of the Plat.

FINAL APPROVAL

The Planning Commission will consider approval of the Final Plat for record only after monuments have been installed in accordance with the specifications given below, and after there has been filed with the City Engineer any of the following certificates or bonds, which, in the opinion of the City Engineer, are required by the public interest:

1. A certificate that all streets shown on the plat have been graded and improved, and that, where required, sewerage and water utilities and facilities have been installed, in accordance with the City's specifications; or

2. A duly completed and executed bond by a Surety Company authorized to execute bonds in the State of . . ., certified by the City Attorney as valid and enforceable by the City in an amount; and with Surety satisfactory to the City Engineer, securing the making and installation of these improvements, utilities and facilities within the period fixed by the City Engineer.

3. The City will not make any improvements to the streets, alleys and other public ways of any subdivision or grant any services to said subdivision unless plat of said subdivision is duly approved as provided herein, and is recorded in the office of the Register of . . . County.

SECTION 13. Appeal.

Any person, firm or corporation may appeal from action of the Planning Commission in failing and refusing to approve any plat or plan submitted under the provisions of this Ordinance within a period of ten (10) days after rejection by the Planning Commission, and the Board of Commissioners, after hearing evidence on behalf of the owner and Planning Commission, may determine whether or not the Planning Commission shall be sustained or overruled.

SECTION 14. Enforcement and Penalties.

1. No plat or plan of the subdivision of land into two or more lots shall be recorded by the County Register of Deeds until said plat or plan has received final approval, in writing, by the Planning Commission.

2. Any person, firm or corporation who violates, disobeys, omits,

neglects or refuses to comply with or who resists the enforcement of any of the provisions of this Ordinance shall be fined not less than two dollars ($2.00) nor more than fifty dollars ($50.00) for each offense. Each day a violation exists shall constitute a separate offense.

SECTION 15. VALIDITY.

Should any Section, clause or provision of this Ordinance be declared to be invalid by a Court of competent jurisdiction the same shall not affect the validity of this Ordinance as a whole or any part thereof other than the part so declared to be invalid.

SECTION 16. CONFLICTS.

1. All Ordinances or parts of Ordinances in conflict herewith or inconsistent with the provisions of this Ordinance, be, and the same are, hereby repealed.
2. These regulations are deemed supplemental to and are to be administered to enhance the administration of Ordinance No . . ., . . . Zoning Ordinance.

SECTION 17. EFFECTIVE DATE.

This Ordinance shall take effect two weeks from and after its passage, the public welfare requiring it.

Reproduced with the kind permission from E.C. Yokley, *Law of Subdivisions,* 2nd ed. (Charlottesville: The Michie Co. 1981) pp. 534-547.

APPENDIX D

Park Dedication Ordinances

KANSAS CITY, MISSOURI

SUBDIVISION REGULATIONS
Chapter 31, Code of General Ordinances

Sec. 31.31. Parks, playgrounds and open space areas.

(a) Definitions. As used in this section 31.32, the following definitions shall apply:

    (1) *Single Family Dedication* shall mean the number of acres calculated by taking the number of single family units to be included in the subdivision and multiplying that number times three and seven-tenths (3.7) people per single family unit and then taking the resulting number and multiplying that number times six one-thousandths (.006) of an acre per person.

    (2) *Duplex Dedication* shall mean the number of acres calculated by taking the number of duplex units to be included in the subdivision and multiplying that number times three (3) people per duplex unit and then taking the resulting number and multiplying that number times six one-thousandths (.006) of an acre per person.

    (3) *Multi-Family Dedication* shall mean the number of acres calculated by taking the number of multi-family units to be included in the subdivision and multiplying that number times two (2) people per multi-family unit and then taking the resulting number and multiplying that number times six one-thousandths (.006) of an acre per person.

    (4) *Required Parkland Dedication* shall mean the number of acres calculated by adding together the Single Family Dedication and the Duplex Dedication and the Multi-Family Dedication, as defined above.

(5) *Current Year's Price,* for any given year, shall mean the following:
  (a) For the calendar year 1979, six thousand dollars ($6,000);
  (b) For all other calendar years, the average cost per acre actually paid by the City for all purchases of tracts of parkland of forty-nine (49) acres or less, whether through negotiation or condemnation but excluding all acquisitions wholly or partially obtained through gift, during the five (5) calendar years immediately preceding said calendar year.

(b) Dedication. Subdivision plats shall show dedication of land for park uses at locations designated in the comprehensive plan, or the official parks plan adopted by the Board of Parks and Recreation Commissioners, or as determined by the subdivider and the staff of City Development and Parks and Recreations Departments, in the amount of the Required Parkland Dedication. When the Required Parkland Dedication is less than four (4) acres, the city plan commission may require the open space to be located at a suitable place of the periphery of the subdivision, so a more usable tract will result when additional open space is obtained when adjacent land is subdivided. In all cases, the developer will dedicate such approved park land to the city for park purposes as a condition of final subdivision approval. All land to be dedicated to the city for park purposes shall have the prior approval of the Board of Parks and Recreation Commissioners, and shall be shown and marked on the plat as *"dedicated to Kansas City, Missouri, for park and recreation purposes,"* and the plat will be so endorsed by the President of the Board of Parks and Recreation Commissioners.

The Board of Parks and Recreation Commissioners shall affix its approval to the plat within three (3) weeks or receipt of the certified legal description for the property from the city engineer. Notwithstanding anything else contained herein, if the subdivider and the staff of City Development and Parks and Recreation Departments are unable to agree upon the location of the land to be dedicated as required hereunder, then as a condition of final subdivision approval the subdivider will pay cash-in-lieu of dedicating land, as required below. Also, notwithstanding anything else contained herein, if the Required Parkland Dedication is less than two (2) acres, then the city at its option, elected at any time prior to approval of the preliminary plat by the plats review committee or the city plan commission based upon the election of the developer, may as a condition of final subdivision approval require the subdivider to pay cash-in-lieu of dedicating land, as required below.

(c) Cash in-lieu-of land dedication. Notwithstanding anything contained in subsection (b) above, the subdivider, at the subdivider's sole option which may be elected at any time prior to approval of the preliminary plat by the plats review committee or the city plan commission based upon the election

120

of the developer, may pay cash-in-lieu of dedicating open space. When the subdivider exercises its option to pay cash-in-lieu of dedicating open space, the subdivider shall deposit with the City Treasurer for the Parks and Recreation Acquisition and/or Development Trust Fund, prior to recording the subdivision plat, a cash payment without recourse or the right of recovery equal to the Required Parkland Dedication multiplied by the current year's price for the calendar year in which the preliminary plat is approved by the plats review committee or in the alternative the city plan commission, less a credit that any land actually dedicated for park purposes bears to the Required Parkland Dedication. Such funds shall be used for the acquisition, development or improvement of a public park generally, within one (1) mile of the periphery of the subdivision for which they were paid by the Parks and Recreation Department as authorized by the City charter.

(d) Private development and operation of park-recreational open space. The applicant may comply with the requirements of this section to furnish land for recreational purposes by providing an area which shall meet the minimum standards as required in section 31.31(b), provided that such area shall be developed and maintained by the subdivider or by the lot owners in the subdivision as private property under a legal arrangement approved by the city counselor as adequate to insure its continued operation and maintenance.

(e) Quality of park sites.
 (1) It is the intent that land designated for park and recreational use be suitable for such use and receive the approval of the director of parks and recreation and the city plan commission.
 (2) If the subdivision is of such magnitude that the allocation for park open space would exceed 10 acres, the determination of one or more parcels shall be made by the staffs of City Development and Parks and Recreation subject to the approval of the city plan commission.
 (3) The park open space parcel shall be a cohesive whole but may be of irregular outline or shape.
 (4) The developer may, with concurrence of the Parks and Recreation Department, make as extensive improvements or provide recreational facilities as he may desire. The developer shall improve the land to be dedicated as follows:
  (a) If the Required Parkland Dedication is four (4) acres or less, provide within the park area (as approved by the city plan commission) a play area of 20,000 square feet with not more than a 4% gradient or which could reasonably be graded to such.
  (b) If the Required Parkland Dedication is nine (9) acres or more, provide a play and game area within the park area of

not less than 85,000 square feet with a maximum gradient of 4% or which could reasonably be graded to such.

(c) If the Required Parkland Dedication is between four (4) acres and nine (9) acres, provide a proportionate share of game area.

(d) Any land within the park area disturbed by construction activity shall have the tilth restored and the soil stabilized by appropriate vegetative cover.

(5) Each park open space shall have frontage on a public street which the city plan commission deems necessary to provide acceptable access to the open space from a public street, taking into account the need for adequate frontage on a public street and the amount of frontage reasonably required by the circumstances of the particular open space. This frontage may serve a corridor from the public street to the main body of the park area which the city plan commission deems necessary to provide acceptable access to the open space from the public street. This corridor shall have a gradient adequate for pedestrian or vehicle use.

(f) Additional recreation reservations. The provisions of this section are minimum standards. None of the subsections above shall be construed as prohibiting a developer from dedicating or reserving other land for recreation purposes in addition to the requirements of this section.

(Comm. Sub. Ordinance 50530, 8-30-79)

Sec. 31.33. Other public uses.

(a) Plat to provide for public uses. The developer shall suitably incorporate into his preliminary plat other public uses as indicated in the official master plan. Other public uses include such as a school, recreation uses in excess of the requirements in section 31.31 or any other similar public uses as indicated by the developer by any provision of the zoning ordinance.

The determination of necessity for acquisition of such other public uses shall be by the city plan commission as part of the development phase in accordance with (b) below. If the determination has been made to acquire the site by the city or other public agency, the site shall be suitably incorporated by the developer into the preliminary plat and final plat.

(b) Referral to public body. The secretary of the city plan commission or his designated representative shall refer the preliminary plat to the public body concerned with the proposed acquisition for its consideration and report. Alternate areas for such acquisition may be proposed. The secretary of the city plan commission shall invite the public body or agency to respond at the Plats Review Committee meeting when this proposal will be discussed. The agency's recommendation, if affirmative, shall include a map showing the boundaries and area of the parcel to be acquired and an estimate of the time required to complete the acquisition.

(c) Notice to property owner. Upon receipt of an affirmative report from item (b) above, the secretary of the city plan commission shall notify the subdivider and shall require designation of the area proposed to be acquired by the city or other public body on the final plat.

(d) Duration of land reservation. The acquisition of the land reserved by the city or other public body on the final plat shall be consummated within twelve (12) months of written notification from the owner that he intends to develop the land. Such letter of intent shall be accompanied by a sketch plat of the proposed development and a tentative schedule of construction. Failure on the part of the city or other public agency to consummate acquisition within the prescribed twelve (12) months shall result in the removal of the reserved designation from the property involved and the freeing of the property for development in accordance with these regulations. The developer shall replat this parcel in accordance with the provisions of these regulations.

(Comm. Sub. Ordinance 50190, 8-30-79)

COLLEGE STATION, TEXAS

Subdivision Regulations

SECTION 10: REQUIREMENTS FOR PARK LAND DEDICATION

10-A. Purpose

10-A.1.
This section is adopted to provide recreational areas in the form of neighborhood parks as a function of subdivision development in the City of College Station. This section is enacted in accordance with the home rule powers of the City of College Station, granted under the Texas Constitution, and the statutes of the State of Texas, including, but not by way of limitation, Articles 974a and 1175. It is hereby declared by the city council that recreational areas in the form of neighborhood parks are necessary and in the public welfare, and that the only adequate procedure to provide for same is by integrating such a requirement into the procedure for planning and developing property or subdivision in the city, whether such development consists of

new construction on vacant land or rebuilding and remodeling of structures on existing residential property.

10-A.2.
Neighborhood parks are those parks providing for a variety of outdoor recreational opportunities and within convenient distances from a majority of the residences to be served thereby. The park zones established by the parks and recreation department and shown on the official parks and recreation map for the City of College Station shall be prima facie proof that any park located therein is within such a convenient distance from any residence located therein. The primary cost of neighborhood parks should be borne by the ultimate residential property owners who, by reason of the proximity of their property to such parks, shall be the primary beneficiaries of such facilities. Therefore, the following requirements are adopted to effect the purposes stated:

10-B. General Requirement, R-1, R-1A, R-2, R-3, R-4, R-5, R-6 Land, to be Used for Single-Family, Duplex, and/or Apartment Residential Purposes

10-B.1.
Whenever a final plat is filed of record with the county clerk of Brazos County for development of a residential area in accordance with the planning and zoning regulations of the city, such plat shall contain a clear fee simple dedication of an area of land to the city for park purposes, which area shall equal one (1) acre for each one hundred thirty-three (133) proposed dwelling units. Any proposed plat submitted to the city for approval shall show the area proposed to be dedicated under this section. The required dedication of this subsection may be met by a payment of money in lieu of land when permitted or required by the other provisions of this section.

10-B.2.
The city council declares that development of an area smaller than one (1) acre for public parks purposes is impractical. Therefore, if fewer than one hundred thirty-three (133) units are proposed by a plat filed for approval, the developer shall be required to pay the applicable cash in lieu of land amount provided by 10-D.3., rather than to dedicate any land area. No plat showing a dedication of less than one (1) acre shall be approved.

10-B.3.
In instances where an area of less than five (5) acres is required to be dedicated, the city shall have the right to accept the dedication for approval on the final plat, or to refuse same, after consideration of the recommendation of the planning and zoning committee and the parks and recreation board, and to require payment of cash in lieu of land in the amount provided by 10-D.3.,

if the city determines that sufficient park area is already in the public domain in the area of the proposed development, or if the recreation potential for that zone would be better served by expanding or improving existing parks.

10-B.4.

The dedication required by this section shall be made by filing of the final plat or contemporaneously by separate instrument unless additional dedication is required subsequent to the filing of the final plat. If the actual number of completed dwelling units exceed the figure upon which the original dedication was based, such additional dedication shall be required, and shall be made by payment of the cash in lieu of land amount provided by 10-D.3., or by the conveyance of an entire numbered lot to the city.

10-C. Prior Dedication; Absence of Prior Dedication

10-C.1.

Credit shall be given for land and/or money dedicated pursuant to Ordinance 690 or 983.

10-C.2.

If a dedication requirement arose prior to the passage of this section, that dedication requirement shall be controlled by the ordinance in effect at the time such obligation arose, except that additional dedication shall be required if the actual density of structures constructed upon the property is greater than the former assumed density. Additional dedication shall be required only for the increase in density and shall be based upon the ratio set forth in 10-B. of this section.

10-C.3.

At the discretion of the city, any former gift of land to the city may be credited on a per acre basis toward eventual land dedication requirements imposed on the donor of such lands. The city council shall consider the recommendation of the planning and zoning commission and the parks and recreation board in exercising its discretion under this subsection.

10-D. Money in Lieu of Land

10-D.1.

Subject to veto of the city council, a land owner responsible for dedication under this section may elect to meet the requirements of 10-B. in whole or in part by a cash payment in lieu of land, in the amount set forth in 10-D.3. Such payment in lieu of land shall be made at or prior to the time of final plat approval.

10-D.2.

The city may from time to time, decide to purchase land for parks in or near the area of actual or potential development. If the city does purchase park land in a park zone, subsequent park land dedications for that zone shall be in cash only, and calculated to reimburse the city's actual cost of acquisition and development of such land for parks. The cash amount shall be equal to the sum of the average price per acre of such land, and the actual cost of adjacent streets and onsite utilities, or an estimate of such actual cost provided by the city engineer. Once the city has been reimbursed entirely for all such park land within a park zone, this subsection shall cease to apply, and the other subsections of this section shall again be applicable.

10-D.3.

To the extent that 10-D.2. is not applicable, the dedication requirement shall be met by a payment in lieu of land at a per- acre price set from time to time by resolution by the city council, sufficient to acquire land and provide for adjacent streets and utilities for a neighborhood park to serve the park zone in which such development is located. Unless changed by the city council, such per-acre price shall be computed on the basis of two hundred twenty-five dollars (225.00) per dwelling unit. Cash payments may be used only for acquisition or improvement of a neighborhood park located within the same zone as the development.

10-E. Comprehensive Plan Considerations

Land shown on a comprehensive plan as being suitable for development of the city for a major recreational center, school site, park, or other public use, shall be reserved for a period of one (1) year after the preliminary plat is approved by the city if within two (2) months after such approval the city council advises the subdivider of its desire to acquire the land or of the interest of another government unit to acquire the land, for purchase by the interested governmental authority at land appraisal value at the time or purchase. A failure by the city council to so notify the subdivider shall constitute a waiver of the right to reserve the land. Any waiver of the right to reserve the land shall no longer be effective if the preliminary plat shall expire without adoption of a final plat.

10-F. Special Fund; Right to Refund

10-F.1.

There is hereby established a special fund for the deposit of all sums paid in lieu of land dedication under this section or any preceding ordinance, which fund shall be known as the park land dedication fund.

10-F.2.

The city shall account for all sums paid in lieu of land dedication under this section with reference to the individual plats involved. Any funds paid for such purposes must be expended by the city within two (2) years from the date received by the city for acquisition of development of a neighborhood park as defined herein. Such funds shall be considered to be spent on a first in, first out basis. If not so expended, the owners of the property on the last day of such period shall be entitled to a prorata refund of such sum, computed on a square footage of area basis. The owners of such property must request such refund within one (1) year of entitlement, in writing, or such right shall be barred.

10-G. Additional Requirements; Definitions

10-G.1.

Any land dedicated to the city under this section must be suitable for park and recreation uses. The following characteristics of a proposed area are generally unsuitable:

(a) Any area primarily located in the 100-year flood plain.
(b) Any areas of unusual topography or slope which renders same unusable for organized recreational activities.

The above characteristics of a park land dedication area may be grounds for refusal of any preliminary plat.

10-G.2.

Drainage areas may be accepted as part of a park if the channel is constructed in accordance with city engineering standards, and if no significant area of the park is cut off from access by such channel.

10-G.3.

Each park must have ready access to a public street.

10-G.4.

Unless provided otherwise herein, an action by the city shall be by the city council, after consideration of the recommendations of the planning and zoning commission and the parks and recreation board. Any proposal considered by the planning and zoning commission under this section shall have been reviewed by the parks and recreation committee and its recommendation given to the commission. The commission may make a decision contrary to such recommendations only by a concurring vote of at least five (5) members. Should the commission be unable to get this vote, the matter shall then be referred to the city council for its decision.

(Ordinance No. 1265 of January 22, 1981)

APPENDIX E

Park Space Standards

Park and recreation space standards have historically been used to (1) establish community park goals or (2) quantitively measure performance. Unfortunately, both have been applied as unrealistic absolutes rather than flexible guidelines. In neither instance are they a qualitative measure of park and recreation services. Measuring municipal park acreages against park standards reveals that the standards are neither feasible nor attainable. The rate of attainment of most American cities is about 25 percent.[1] Despite warnings about universal application of standards and the need for flexibility why have planners used them as a crutch? First, most standards are simple, allowing decision makers to quickly apply them as a solution to a problem. Second, they are drafted by national organizations, such as the NRPA, and as such are legitimized as the experts rule. Third, they represent a prestigious ideal and are used for status comparisons. Lastly, they are used as a bargaining justification in the community budgetary process.[2]

The origin of park standards is obscure and shrouded in history. Their birth can be traced to the 1890's, to the foundation of the recreation movement.[3] The National Recreation and Park Society has described this genesis as:

> Quite early in the century some proposed that a municipality should provide ten (10) acres of recreation space per thousand of the population. The actual origin of this standard is not known; however the National Recreation Association accepted and promoted it as desired standard.[4]

In tracing the development of park standards during this period, Kjelte and Shivers, two recreation researchers concluded:

> . . . that these standards or ratio was never based upon any factual knowledge of validated scientific analysis. It was, and is a historical estimate of expert opinion, which was developed in another country in 1900. No valid standards exist for the acquisition and development of recreational spaces in urban centres and metropolitan regions. The only standards are those inconsistent estimate and guess, and these vary with local conditions.[5]

And so this best guestimate of unknown and untested expert opinion was adopted by the National Recreation Association (NRA). In 1933 the NRA, the predecessor to NRPA, updated the standards and they have, with minor modification, remained the same today. Despite the caveat that the standards were merely a guide, they have become widely accepted as the rule. This acceptance increased the standards' authority and encouraged other communities to accept them without revision or question.

There are three types of park standards currently used by municipalities: *size, location* and *use*. Size standards are based upon the area of the site per population often expressed as a percentage of the total area standard. For example, 10 percent of the land area in a new subdivision being allocated to parks. A variation of this approach relates acreage to population. For example, two acres of neighborhood park per 1000 population. Use standards are based upon the type of recreation to be provided by a given facility. For example, a neighborhood playground is intended to primarily serve children 3 to 26 years of age whereas a community park may serve clientele from 3 to 50 years of age. Location standards are based upon a service radii concept delineating the geographical distances people are expected to travel to a particular park. For example, a playground within 1/2 mile of all households within a given subdivision.

A litany of criticisms have been raised by writers regarding the space standards approach to park planning. Most of this discussion focuses on the shortcomings of the standards in failing to consider local conditions. Despite all of these warnings there does not appear to be a widely accepted alternative to quantifying the amount and type of park space required to provide a quality recreation service. Refining these space standards would require the incorporation of citizens needs and preferences (needs assessment) in the formulation of new contemporary community standards. Such an approach, building on the historical basis of space standards but incorporating contemporary needs, is a legally defensible approach whose time has come. The unilateral adoption of the NRPA standard without incorporating contemporary community needs is an approach whose time is past.

The classification system of parks presented in this section uses the terminology most commonly found within the park and recreation profession in the United States in 1982.[6] In addition to traditional resources, there are a host of special-purpose park and recreation resources, such as theme parks, historic parks, battlefield parks, waterfront parks, riverwalk parks, athletic parks, aquatic parks, and cultural parks, and living history communities. Because of this potential diversity, it is important in developing community park and recreation space standards that recognition be given first to the provision of space for basic park and recreation needs. Other lands and special purpose resources extend beyond the basic minimum acreage to enhance and diversify the opportunities available to the community.

A PARKS TYPOLOGY[7]

This classification system is intended to serve as a guide to planning and not as an absolute blueprint. Sometimes more than one component may occur within the same site (but not on the same parcel of land), particularly with respect to special uses within a regional park. Planners of park and recreation systems should be careful to provide adequate land for each functional component when this occurs.

NRPA suggests that a park system, at a minimum, be composed of a "core" system of parklands, with a total of 6.25 to 10.5 acres of developed open space per 1,000 population. The size and amount of "adjunct" parklands will vary from community to community, but must be taken into account when considering a total, well-rounded system of parks and recreation areas.

I. Mini-Park

1. Description: Small areas intended primarily for the use of children up to the early elementary grades in high density areas.
2. Contents: Play apparatus, swings, slides, sandboxes, paved areas for wheeled toys, benches, wading or spray pools, landscape treatment.
3. Population served: In general terms, serves ages toddlers to nine. Playlots should be combined with adult gathering areas. Usually a part of the park system of urban areas with a minimum of 10,000 population.
4. Service area and accessibility: The service area is confined to the sub-neighborhood level from 500 to 2,500 persons within a 1/4-mile radius.

II. Neighborhood Park

1. Description: Designed to provide both active and passive short-term activities. Neighborhood playgrounds are, quite often, adjacent to public school sites. May contain scenic and aesthetic resources.
2. Contents: Distinct play areas for both pre-school and school age children, storage and shelter structures, some open space for spontaneous play, multiple-use paved areas for court games, areas for field games with possible limited seating for spectators, wading and spray pool, game area for adults such as shuffleboard or horseshoes, etc., possible outdoor ice rinks, landscaped perimeter buffers, some off-street parking, lighting. Passive areas include open lawn or wooded areas.
3. Population served: For all ages, but focuses on 5-39 with emphasis upon ages 5-18. From 1,000 to 10,000 maximum.

4. Service area and accessibility: Neighborhood; within 1/2-mile radius. Easy walking distance. If park is unique, it may attract others from another neighborhood.

III. Community Park

1. Description: A large natural and/or landscaped area to provide the urban dweller with a pleasurable reprieve from the congestion of the city without having to travel a great distance. Designed to accommodate large numbers of people for a wide variety of day uses. Provides for both intensive uses and passive pursuits.
2. Content: Provides for combination of intensive and non-intensive development ranging from play apparatus to bicycle trails. Some typical facilities included swimming, beach or pool, picnic tables, paths, game courts, gardens and natural areas, ice skating, winter sports, pavilion, golf, zoo or museums, ample parking, sanitary facilities. May include nature trails, trails for the physically and visually disabled, as well as bicycle trails internally as part of a larger system. May also be a feature along a larger trail system.
3. Population served: All ages, toddler to retiree. Usually serves between 40,000 persons up to 100,000.
4. Service area and accessibility: Entire population for cities with population up to 25,000
   1-4 miles=Cities of 1,000-25,000
   within 30 minutes=25,000-250,000+

IV. Special Purpose Facility

1. Description: The chief feature may be uniqueness such as a marina, zoo, concert bowl (Hollywood bowl), or some other special characteristics. Included may be festivals (Tulip, Cherry Blossom). Also, items of historical significance such as Greenfield Village and Mackinac Island.
2. Contents: All age groups depending upon function and purpose, e.g., a children's zoo is primarily for ages toddler to nine, whereas candle making, such as may be seen at Greenfield Village, is for ages probably over 15 without an upper limit. Vary depending upon the unit. Usually includes sanitary facilities. May be a feature or event along a trail, a linear or historical segment of trail, or function as an integral part of a trail.
3. Population served: Entire regional or state population. May attract population from a much larger base.
4. Service area and accessibility: Multi-county or multi-municipal or

both. Probably serves a population within three hours travel time, but may have a wider appeal.

V. Urban Greenspace

1. Description: Passive areas in landscaped or natural state in or near urban areas. May be planned for conversion to more intensive recreational uses when needed. May provide recreational uses when needed. May provide recreational experiences, provide environmental quality, or act as buffers. Main recreational purpose is to break-up atmosphere of congestion and provide aesthetic experience. Also can act as land bank system (see 2 below).
2. Contents: Natural lands, watershed and waterfront, forests, landscaped borders, parkways and boulevards, corner parks, medians, downtown aesthetic parks, plazas, malls, sanitary facilities. Can provide bicycle, hiking, nature, or bridle trail system as a feature or as part of a larger system.
3. Population served: Entire population, but may also be used as privacy buffer against high-traffic corridors.
4. Service area and accessibility: Not established. Often considered a part of the parks system and viewed as part of urban beautification program. Primary accessibility is visual although some hiking paths are located in a few greenbelt greenspace areas along traffic corridors.

VI. Regional Park

1. Description: Serves multi-governmental units and usually administered by counties or regional bodies. Many recreation activities are associated with experiencing the natural environment. Located for good access from major roads. Normally available for both day and overnight use. Some purposes served are preservation of portion of natural landscape, provision of extensive recreational facilities in urban areas, and service as greenbelts in metropolitan regions.
2. Contents: Parking, picnic areas, nature centers, trail systems, scenic drives, campgrounds, water areas for swimming and boating, golf courses, botanical gardens, possible miniature train, winter sport areas, concession facilities and sanitary facilities, and in some cases, sport fields. Often serves as an integral part of a trail system including hiking and possibly overnight trail camping, or may contain the entire trail. May also function as a trail feature.
3. Population served: All age groups. Entire population of the region.
4. Service area and accessibility: Multi-county and/or multi-city; services mainly those within an hour's travel time radius.

APPENDIX E FOOTNOTES

1. S.M. Gold, *Urban Recreation Planning,* (Philadelphia: Lea and Febiger, 1973) p. 145.
2. R.C. Young, *Elements of Outdoor Recreation Planning,* ed. B.L. Driver (Ann Arbor, Mich: Univ. of Michigan, 1970), p. 262.
3. For a scholarly discussion of the history of recreation space standards see Theobold, *A History of Recreation Resource Planning: The Origins of Space Standards,* 3 Leisure Studies, 189 (1984) and Wilkinson, *The Golden Fleece: the Search for Standards,* 4 Leisure Studies 189 (1985).
4. Outdoor Recreation Space Standards (Arlington, Va: National Recreation and Parks Assoc. 1976), p. 5.
5. G. Hjelte, and J. Shivers, *Planning Recreation Places,* (Cranbury, NJ: Fairleigh Dickinson University Press, 1971), p. 210.
6. R. Lancaster, ed., *Recreation, Park and Open Space Standards and Guidelines* (Arlington, Va: National Recreation and Park Assoc. 1983), p. 55.
7. Ibid, pp. 56-90.

Table AE-1. Neighborhood Park Guidelines.

Agency	Acres/1000 Pop.	Service Area	Recommended Park Size (acres)
Large Cities (>500,000 population)			
Austin, Texas	2.0	1/2 mile	6-10
Baltimore, Maryland	1.0	1/2 mile	—
Dade County, Fla. (Miami)	1.25	1/2 mile	7
Dallas, Texas	1.0	1/2 mile	3-6
Kansas City, Miss.	6.0	—	5-15
Los Angeles, Calif.	4.0	1/2 mile	10
Medium Cities (< 500,000 population)			
Des Moines, Iowa	1.25	1/2 mile	5-7
Greensboro, N. Carol.	1.5	1 mile	—
Lubbock, Texas	2.0	1/2 mile	3 (minimum)

Oklahoma City, Okla.	2.0	—	5-10

Small Cities (<75,000 population)

Alpena, Michigan	5.0	1/2 mile	5-10
Billings, Mont.	2.5	—	—
College Station, Texas	1.0		5-15
Elmhurst, Illinois	3.0	1/4 mile	5-10

Other

NRPA	2.0	1/2 mile	15

APPENDIX F

Bibliography of Law Reviews

I. SUBDIVISION CONTROLS AND EXACTIONS

Harvith. "Subdivision Dedication Requirements—Some Observations and an Alternative: A Special Tax on Gain from Realty." *Albany Law Review* 33 (1969): 474.

Jacobson. "Expropriation by Forced Dedication." *Journal of Beverly Hills Bar Association* 6 (1972): 10.

Rundus, Jan. "The Permissible Scope of Compulsory Requirements for Land Development in Colorado." *University of Colorado Law Review* 54 (1983):447-468.

Reps. "Control of Land Subdivision by Municipal Planning Boards." *Cornell Law Quarterly* 49 (1955):258.

Johnston. "Constitutionality of Subdivision Control Exactions: The Quest for a Rationale." *Cornell Law Quarterly* 52 (1967):871.

Freese. "Subdivision Regulations and Compulsory Dedications." *Dicta* 39 (1962):299.

Note. "Dedication: Rights Under Misurer and Alienation of Lands Dedicated to Specific Municipal Purposes." *University of Florida Law Review* 7 (1954):82.

Note. "Land Subdivision Control." *Harvard Law Review* 65 (1952):1226.

Taylor. "Current Problems in California Subdivision Control." *Hastings Law Journal* 13 (1962):344.

Note. "Forced Dedications." *Hastings Law Journal* 20(1969):735.

Curtin. "Requiring Dedication of Land by Developers." *Institute on Planning, Zoning, and Eminent Domain* 57 (1974):79. Southwest Legal Foundation.

Hamilton. "Dedication Requirements-Binding Conditions or Inverse Condemnation." *Institute on Planning, Zoning, and Eminent Domain* 89 (1977). Southwest Legal Foundation.

Staples. "Exaction—Mandatory Dedication and Payments in Lieu of Dedication." *Institute on Plan, Zoning & Eminent Domain.* 111 (1980). Southwest Legal Foundation.

Note. "An Analysis of Subdivision Control Legislation." *Indiana Law Journal* 28 (1953):544.

Note. "Subdivision Regulation in Iowa." *Iowa Law Review.* 54 (1969):1121.

Yearwood. "Accepted Controls of Land Subdivision." *Journal of Urban Law* 45(1967):217.

Pavelko, Thomas. "Subdivision Exactions: a Review of Judicial Standards." *Journal of Urban and Contemporary Law* 25 (1983):269.

Adelstein, R.P. and Edelsen, N.M. "Subdivision Exactions and Congestion Externalities." *Journal of Legal Studies* 5 (1978):147.

Cunningham. "Public Control of Land Subdivision in Michigan." *Michigan Law Review* 66 (1967):1.

Curtin, Daniel J., Jr. "Park Land Dedication or Fees in Lieu Thereof: A Legal Innovation for Parkland Acquisition and Development." *The Municipal Attorney* 10 (May-June 1969): 74.

Note. "Platting, Planning & Protection—a Summary of Subdivision Statutes." *New York Univ. Law Review* 36 (1961):1205.

Note. "Subdivision Exactions": "Where is the Limit?" *Notre Dame Law Review* 42 (1967):400.

Note. "Dedication v. Condemnation—Constitutionality of Planning Commission Requirements." *Oklahoma Law Review* 29 (1976):155.

Ferguson, Jerry T. and Rasnic, Carol D. "Judicial Limitations on Mandatory Subdivision Dedications." *Real Estate Law Journal* 13 (1984):250.

Note. "Forced Dedications as a Condition to Subdivision Approval." *San Diego Law Review.* 9(1971):112.

Ledbetter. "Subdivision Control in South Carolina." *South Carolina Law Review* 24 (1972):155.

Note. "Land Subdivision Regulation: Its Effects And Constitutionality." *St. John's Law Review* 41 (1967):374.

Note. "Subdivision Land Dedications: Objectives and Objections." *Stanford Law Review* 27 (1975):419.

Reps. and Smith. "Control of Urban Land Subdivisions." *Syracuse Law Review* 14 (1963):405.

Hudee, Albert J. "Municipal Exactions and the Subdivision Approval Process: A Legal and Economic Analysis." *University of Toronto Faculty Law Review* 38 (1980):106.

Armbrust. "Platmail: Permissible and Impermissible Requirements in the Subdivision Process." *University of Texas Mortgage Lending Institute* (1984):12.

Note. "Development Fees: Standards to Determine Reasonableness." *Utah Law Review* 59 (1982):549.

Comment. "Money Payment Requirements as Conditions to the Approval of Subdivision Maps: Analysis and Prognosis." *Villanova Law Review* 9 (1964):294.

Comment. "Subdivision Exactions: the Constitutional Issues, the Judicial Response and the Pennsylvania Situation." *Villanova Law Review* 19 (1974):782.

Note. "Subdivision Exactions: a Review of Judicial Standards." *Washington Urban and Contemporary Law* 25 (1983):269.

Cutler. "Legal and Illegal Methods of Controlling Growth on the Urban Fringe." *Wisconsin Law Review.* (1961):370.

Heyman, Ira M. and Gilhool, Thomas K. "The Constitutionality of Imposing Increased Community Costs on New Suburban Residents through Subdivision Exactions." *Yale Law Journal* 73 (1964):1119.

Ellickson. "Suburban Growth Controls: An Economic and Legal Analysis." *Yale Law Journal* 86 (1977):385.

Sax. "Takings and the Police Power." *Yale Law Journal* 74 (1964):36.

II. PARK LAND OR FEE EXACTIONS

Karp, James P. "Subdivision Exactions for Park and Open Space Needs." *American Business Law Journal* 16 (1979):277.

Note. "Mandatory Dedication for Park and Recreation Facilities." *Arkansas Law Review* 26 (1972):415.

Note. "Municipalities: Validity of Subdivision Fees for Schools and Parks." *Columbia Law Review* 66 (1966):974.

Landau. "Urban Concentration and Land Exactions for Recreational Use: Some Constitutional Problems in Mandatory Dedication Ordinances in Iowa." *Drake Law Review* 22 (1972):71.

Note. "Technique for Preserving Open Spaces" *Harvard Law Review* 75 (1962):1622.

Note. "Required Dedication of Parkland: An Unconstitutional Taking In Texas." *Houston Law Review* 19 (1981):175.

Woodall, S. Roy, "Mandatory Dedication of Playgrounds and Parks In Residential Subdivisions." *Kentucky Law Journal* 50 (1962):614.

Note. "Constitutional Law—Mandatory Subdivision Exactions for Park and Recreational Purposes." *Missouri Law Review* 43 (1978):582.

Feldman, Harry H. "Recreation Areas in New Subdivisions." *Ohio Cities and Villages* 10 (1962):28.

Dolbeare. "Mandatory Dedication of Public Sites as a Condition in the Subdivision Process in Virginia." *University of Richmond Law Review* 9 (1975):435.

Note. "Los Altos: Reconsidering the Parkland Dedication Exaction." *Stanford Environmental Annual* 82 (1982): 104.

Aycock and Bray. "Constitutionality of Requiring Park Dedication as a Condition of Plat Approval." *Texas Bar Journal* (1982):721.

Note. "Municipal Ordinance Requiring Parkland Dedication as a Condition to Subdivision Plat Approval Held not Unconstitutional Per Se: City of College Station v. Turtle Rock Corporation." *Texas Tech Law Review* 16 (1985):1015.

Volpert, Richard S. "Creation and Maintenance of Open Space in Subdivisions: Another Approach." *UCLA Law Review* 12 (1965):830.

Platt and Maloney-Merkle. "Municipal Improvisations: Open Space Exactions in the Land of Pioneer Trust." *Urban Law* 5 (1973):706.

Note. "Subdivision Regulation: Requiring Dedication of Park Land or Payment of Fees as a Condition Precedent to Plat Approval." *Wisconsin Law Review* (1961):310.

III. IMPACT FEES

Boyd. "Florida Needs a Statewide Impact Fee." *Florida Environmental and Urban Issues* 2 (1974):3.

Juergensmeyer, Julian. "Drafting Impact Fees to Alleviate Florida's Pre-Platted Lands Dilemma." *Florida Environmental and Urban Issues* 7 (1980):7.

Juergensmeyer, Julian and Robert Blake, "Impact Fees: An Answer to Local Governments Capital Funding Dilemma." *Florida State University Law Review* 9 (1981):415.

Currier, Barry, "Legal and Practical Problems Associated With Drafting Impact Ordinances." *Institute on Planning Zoning and Eminent Domain* (1984): 273 Southwest Legal Foundation.

Rhodes, "Impact Fees: The Cost Benefit Dilemma in Florida." *Land Use and Zoning Law Digest* 27 (1975): 7.

Mercer, L. and W. Morgan, "The Relative Efficiency and Reserve Potential of Local User Charges: The California Case." *National Tax Journal* 36 (1983): 203.

Downing, Paul and James, Frank, "Recreational Impact Fees: Characteristics and Current Usage." *National Tax Journal* 36 (1983):477.

Jacobsen, Fred and Jeff Redding, "Impact Taxes: Making Development Pay Its

Way." *N. Carolina Law Review* 55 (1977): 407.

Gougelman. "Impact Fees: National Perspectives to Florida Practice: A Review of Mandatory Land Dedications and Impact Fees that Affect Land Developments." *Nova Law Journal* 4 (1980):137.

Note, "Development Fees: Standards to Determine Their Reasonableness." *Utah Law Review,* 1982 (1982):549.

Note, "Subdivision Exactions in Washington: Impact Fee Controversy." *Washington Law Review* 59 (1984): 289.

Bosselman, Fred and Nancy Strouds, "Pariah to Paragon: Developer Exactions in Florida 1975-85." *Stetson Law Review,* XIV (1985): 527.

Other Books from Venture Publishing

Recreation and Leisure: Issues In An Era of Change, Revised Edition, edited by Thomas L. Goodale and Peter A. Witt.

Leisure In Your Life: An Exploration, Revised Edition, by Geoffrey Godbey.

Recreation Planning and Management, edited by Stanley R. Leiber and Daniel R. Fesenmaier.

Marketing Parks and Recreation, by the National Park Service.

Vandalism Control Management for Parks and Recreation Area, by Monty L. Christiansen.

Winning Support for Parks and Recreation, by the National Park Service.

Values and Leisure and Trends in Leisure Services, by the Academy of Leisure Sciences.

Playing, Living, Learning—A Worldwide Perspective on Children's Opportunities to Play, by Cor Westland and Jane Knight.

Leadership and Administration of Outdoor Pursuits, by Phyllis Ford and James Blanchard.

Private and Commercial Recreation, edited by Arlin Epperson.

Sport and Recreation: An Economic Analysis, by Gratton and Taylor (Distributed for E. and F.N. Spon, Ltd.).

Park Ranger Handbook, by J.W. Shiner.

INDEX

Access to park land, 25, 70-71, 89
Acreage standards (see Park land)
Adjacent infrastructure, 79
Admiral Development Corp. v. City of Maitland, 31, 35, 41, 102
Advance acquisition, 86-87
Agricultural land, 10, 12, 16, 89
Alabama, 33, 101, 105
Alaska, 105
Albuquerque, New Mexico, 95-97
American Law Institute, 98
Annexation, 51, 63, 86, 88
"Arbitrary and capricious", 4, 13, 39, 57
Arizona, 105
Arkansas, 39, 101, 105
Associated Home Builders of Greater East Bay, Inc. v. City of Walnut Creek, 33, 37-38, 39, 45, 101
Aunt Hack Ridge Estates, Inc. v. City of Danbury, 32, 35, 42, 101
Austin, Texas, 54-58, 70, 73-74
Ayers v. City Council of City of Los Angeles, 30

Baker v. City of Milwaukee, 61
Banberry Development Corp. v. South Jordan City, 45, 46
Bargain sale, 87
Beardall Park, 94-95
Berg Development v. City of Missouri City, 104

Bethlehem Evangelical Lutheran Church v. City of Lakewood, 30, 32
Billings Properties Inc. v. Yellowstone Co., 32, 35, 37, 42, 103
Bloomington, Minnesota, 66-67, 79, 84
Board of Education of DuPage Co. v. Surety Developers Inc., 32, 45
Bonds, 84, 98
Borough (see Municipality)
Breckenridge, Colorado, 99
Broward County, Florida, 67
Broward Co. v. Janis Development Corp., 32, 102
Building codes (see Codes)
Building permits (see Permits)

California, 1, 4, 30, 31, 33, 37-38, 39, 45, 51-54, 61, 65, 69-70, 72, 77-78, 101, 105
Call v. City of West Jordan, 31, 32, 38, 41, 104
Capital gains, 10
Capital improvement fee, 83, 85
"Capricious" (see "Arbitrary and capricious")
Carrying capacity, 70
Cash payment (see Fees-in-lieu)
Certificate of occupancy, 15
Cincinnati, Ohio, 30
Citizen participation, 52, 54 (see

also Public hearings)
City (see Municipality)
City charter (see Municipal charter)
City of College Station v. Turtle Rock Corp., 30, 32, 37-38, 43, 45, 92, 104
City of Colorado Springs v. Kitty Hawk Dev. Corp., 101
City council (see Municipal council)
City of Fayetteville v. IBI Inc., 39, 101
City manager, 52
City of Mequon v. Lake Estates Co., 104
City of Montgomery v. Crossroads Land Co., 33, 101
City plan (see Comprehensive plan)
Clean Water Act, 15
Cluster development, 24-25, 85-86, 92
Coalition for Los Angeles County Planning in the Public Interest v. Board of Superiors for Los Angeles County, 61
Codding Enterprises v. City of Merced, 101
Codes:
  building, 8, 15, 18, 99
  development, 61, 64, 89, 98-99
  housing, 15, 84, 99
College Station, Texas, 30, 38, 43, 75-76
Collis v. City of Bloomington, 32, 37, 42, 102
Colorado, 30, 32, 99, 101, 105
Community development plan (see Comprehensive plan)
Compensation (see Private property, taking of)
Comprehensive plan, 9, 50-62
  authority for, 9, 13, 31, 59-60
  and combined planning/

management system, 51-54
  conservation and resources element, 52, 60
  consistency with regulations, 4, 18, 26, 38-9, 47, 57, 60-62, 64, 65, 66
  definitions, 9, 50-51
  and development codes, 98-99
  importance of, 4, 38-40
  as a legal document, 60-61
  as a management tool, 51
  monitoring of, 52, 57
  open space element, 52, 57, 60-61, 88-90, 93, 95, 99
  park and recreation element, 4, 9, 18, 39, 47, 50, 52-62, 64, 65, 66, 75, 80, 83, 88, 93, 99
  as a policy guide, 9, 50-51
  regulatory effect, 9
  standards, 39-40, 50, 52, 54, 57, 66, 98-99
  and zoning, 9, 13, 26, 39, 51, 60-61
Condemnation (see Eminent domain)
Condominiums, 84-85
Connecticut, 31, 32, 33, 35, 42, 101, 105
Conservation (see Environmental protection; Historic sites)
Constitution, 4, 12, 13, 29, 30
Construction, 15, 91
Contracts, 17, 77, 95
Conveying titles, 16
Coronado Development Co. v. City of McPherson, 33, 38, 45, 102
Corpus Christi, Texas, 79
Cost of living index, 81
Cost shifting, 1, 2, 16, 34, 63, 97
Coulter v. City of Rawlins, 31, 32, 38, 44, 104
County, 17, 60 (see also Municipality)
Covenants, 17, 86

Georgia, 102, 105
Gorden v. Village of Wayne, 102
Grants, 84
Greenspace, 133 (see also Open space)

Haugen v. Gleason, 33, 44, 103
Hawaii, 31, 33, 105
Health, safety and welfare, 4, 9, 13, 20, 63, 64, 92
Highest and best use, 12
Hillis Homes Inc. v. Snohomish Co., 32, 45, 104
Hirsch v. City of Mountain View, 30, 101
Historic sites, 12, 16, 64
Hollywood Inc. v. Broward Co., 31, 32, 43, 45, 102
Home Builders Assoc. of Greater Kansas City v. City of Kansas City, 32, 38, 42, 43, 102
Homeowners' associations, 77, 85-86, 92
Home rule, 3, 29, 30-31, 47, 59
Horizontal equity, 46
Housing codes (see Codes)
Houston, Texas, 82

Idaho, 105
Illinois, 1, 4, 32, 34-35, 45, 72-3, 76, 88, 102, 105
Impact fees (see Development impact fees)
Implied authority rule, 31-34
Indiana, 105
Industrial development (see Non-residential development)
Infrastructure costs, 79
Infrastructure services, 51
In re Lake Secor Dev. Co., 103
Iowa, 105

J.E.D. Assoc. Inc. v. Town of Atkinson, 35, 41, 103

Jenad Inc. v. Village of Scarsdale, 32, 36, 103
Jordan v. Village of Menomonee Falls, 31, 32, 36-37, 45, 104

Kambi v. Planning Board of Yorktown, 103
Kansas, 33, 38, 45, 46, 102, 105
Kansas City, Missouri, 76, 89
Kebler v. City of Upland, 101
Kentucky, 105
Krughoff v. City of Naperville, 35, 88, 102

Land conservancy, 87, 89, 93
Land development plan, 98-99
Land speculation, 12
Land trust (see Land conservancy)
Land-use control, 2, 8, 9, 10, 13, 15, 26, 98-99 (see also Mandatory dedication; Subdivision control)
Land-use plan (see Comprehensive plan)
Largo, Florida, 72
Leasing of land, 87
Leisure services (see Parks)
Levin v. Livingston Township, 103
Lien, 87
Life tenancy, 87
Local government (see Municipality)
Lot equalization fee, 45
Louisiana, 105

McKain v. Toledo City Planning Commission, 35, 45
Maine, 105
Maintenance:
  private parks and open space, 77, 85
  public parks, 63, 70, 71, 80, 92
Major statistical area, 79
Mandatory dedication (see also

45, 50, 52-57, 61, 65, 77, 85-86,
88-89, 95-97, 131-133 (see also
Comprehensive plan; Parks;
Sensitive land)
  aggregation of, 95-97
  as different from parks, 64,
    65-66, 86, 93
  industrial needs, 54
  regional, 54, 90, 93
Oregon, 33, 44, 61, 103, 106
Orlando, Florida, 94-95
Park and recreation staff, 8, 17,
  52, 65, 70, 80, 82-83, 92, 95
Park and recreation board, 9, 51,
  77, 83, 91, 93
Park and recreation plan (see
  Comprehensive plan)
Park land:
  acreage standards, 5, 20-23, 38,
    40-44, 47, 66-70, 80, 130
    fixed percentage formula,
      40-42, 66-67
    history of, 129-130
    population-based formula,
      42-44, 67-70
  development schedule, 5, 17, 78
  direct acquisition, 26, 75, 87
  exchange, 93-95
  sale of, 93-95
  site selection
    criteria, 5, 39, 57, 65, 70-71,
      99
    evaluation, 17, 65, 70-71
    standards, 22, 57, 99
    timing, 17, 24, 78, 86
  site management, 91
Parks (see also Open space; Park
  land):
  attitudes towards, 92
  Beardall Park, 94-95
  classification, 22, 57, 130-133
  community, 66, 92, 93, 132
  facilities, 66, 84, 92, 93
  greenline, 93

metropolitan, 93
mini-park, 131
neighborhood, 2, 22, 26, 54, 65,
  66, 82, 92, 93, 131-132
private (see Private parks)
proximity, 22, 70, 74, 75
regional, 93, 131, 133
school, 66, 80
special purpose, 66, 130,
  132-133
Park service area, 75
Parkway system, 90
Patenaude v. Town of Meredith, 32,
  103
Payment in lieu (see Fees in lieu)
Pennsylvania, 1, 106
Permits:
  building, 15, 97
  environmental, 15
  special development, 64
Perpetual management contract,
  17, 77
*Pioneer Trust and Savings Bank v.
  Village of Mount Prospect,*
  34-36, 102
Plan (see Comprehensive plan;
  Neighborhood plan; Plat)
Planned Unit Development (PUD),
  24, 85-86
Planners, 8, 9, 17, 52, 62, 70, 80
Planning and zoning legislation, 3
Planning commission, 5, 8, 9, 16,
  19-20, 30, 31, 36-37, 40, 51,
  65, 70, 78, 83, 91, 92, 93
Planning process, 9, 57-59
Plat:
  approval, 2, 6, 16-17, 19, 20,
    24, 29, 63-65, 86
  compliance with comprehensive
    plan, 18, 19, 64-65
  exemptions, 83
  filing, 5
  final, 5, 17, 20, 78
  preapplication phase, 18

plan; Park land):
design, 2, 88
facility, 54
location, 130
performance, 99
for plat approval, 18
safety, 2, 88
size, 130
space, 22-23, 54, 57, 129
use, 130
Storm drains (see Public facilities)
Streets, 2, 14, 18 (see also Public
facilities)
Subdivision control, 2, 8, 14,
16-20, 26 (see also Enabling
acts, Land-use control,
Mandatory dedication, Plat)
authority for, 3, 5, 29
benefits, 16
and comprehensive plan, 4, 18,
26, 38-39, 47, 57, 60-62, 64,
65, 66
history, 2, 9, 14, 16, 29
legislation, 5
judicial doctrine, 4-5
ordinance, 2, 26-27, 30, 63-81,
89, 98, 107-119
purpose of, 2, 14, 16
standards, 2, 16, 20, 26, 57, 63
and zoning, 14, 98-99
Suburbs, 1
Sunbelt states, 1
Sunnyvale, California, 51-54
Supreme Court (see U.S. Supreme
Court)

Taking of private property (see
Private property, taking of)
Taxes, 10-12, 24, 25
Taxation, 1, 10, 12, 26, 60, 89
Tax base sharing, 83-84
TDR (see Transfer of development
rights)
Tennessee, 106

Texas, 1, 5, 30, 32, 37-38, 43, 45,
54-58, 70, 73-73, 75-76, 82-3,
104, 106
Time-price differential, 46
*Town of Longboat Key v. Lands
End Ltd.*, 43, 45, 102
Township (see Municipality)
Trails, 71, 85
Transfer of development rights
(TDR), 15-16, 89
Trees, 90, 91
*Trent Meredith, Inc. v. City of
Oxnard,* 101
Trust funds, 74

"Ultra vires," 4, 13
U.S. Supreme Court, 3, 8, 34
Urban fringe, 10, 12
Urban sprawl, 8
Use valuation, 12, 89
Utah, 5, 31, 32, 38, 41, 45, 46,
67, 97, 104, 106
Utilities, 71 (see also Public
facilities)
Utility corridors (see Public
facilities)

Vermont, 31, 33, 106
Village (see Municipality)
*Village of Euclid v. Ambler Realty
Co.,* 8
Virginia, 104, 106

Walnut Creek, California, 65,
69-70, 77-78
Washington, 32, 45, 104
Watercourses, 15, 70, 89, 91
Water lines (see Public facilities)
Welfare (see Health, safety and
welfare)
West Jordan, Utah, 67
*West Park Ave. v. Township of
Ocean,* 33, 88
West Virginia, 106